Tony D Triggs

GERMANY Between The WARS

Hitler and the Third Reich

Oliver & Boyd

Introduction

This book presents a fascinating chapter in recent history, using photographs, comments, accounts and cartoons which appeared at the time. The sectioning and questions make these documents accessible to the widest possible range of pupils, helping them to understand the nature of each piece of evidence and to use it with discernment and discrimination. The focus is on the skills and sensitive awareness which are at a premium both for the GCSE and Scottish Standard Grade assessments.

Tony D Triggs

Oliver & Boyd
Longman House
Burnt Mill, Harlow
Essex CM20 2JE

An Imprint of Longman Group UK Ltd

© Oliver & Boyd 1990

ISBN 0 05 004384 6

First published 1990

Set in 10/11 Helvetica and 11/13 Palatino by
Word Power, Edinburgh

Produced by Longman Group (F.E.) Ltd
and printed in Hong Kong

Contents

1   The Kaiser

'We cannot make good the severe losses we have suffered in battle. We cannot force peace on the enemy. With each passing day, conditions deteriorate. The fighting must be broken off.' The German Field Marshall Paul von Hindenburg wrote this to the German Kaiser (Emperor) on 29 September 1918. Germany's principal enemies were France and Great Britain. After four years of trench warfare, mainly in northern France, French and British soldiers were now defeating the Germans. The conflict, known as the First World War, was nearing its end.

At the time of the War, Germany consisted of separate states (sometimes called *lander*) which were largely self-ruling. The Kaiser, Wilhelm II, belonged to the ancient Hohenzollern family; he was more important than the regional ruler, for he bound the country together. However, he had some serious faults. For example, he was not very tactful. In 1908 (six years before the outbreak of War) a British journalist interviewed him, and this is part of what he said:

Source 1.3   Englishmen, in giving the rein to suspicions unworthy of a great nation, [are as] mad as March hares... My heart is set upon peace, and ... it is one of my dearest wishes to live on the best of terms with England.

My task is not of the easiest. The prevailing sentiment among large sections of the middle and lower classes of my own people is not friendly to England. I am therefore, so to speak, in a minority in my own land... That is another reason why I resent your refusal to accept my pledged word that I am the friend of England...

POKER AND TONGS;
OR, HOW WE'VE GOT TO PLAY THE GAME.

KAISER. "I GO THREE DREADNOUGHTS."
JOHN BULL. "WELL, JUST TO SHOW THERE'S NO ILL-FEELING, I RAISE YOU THREE."

Source 1.1

Cartoons which appeared in Britain during the latter part of the Kaiser's reign

Source 1.2

Germany would always keep aloof from politics that could bring her into complications with a sea power like England...

Germany looks ahead. She must be prepared for any eventualities in the Far East. Who can foresee what may take place in the Pacific in the days to come? ... Only those powers which have great navies will be listened to with respect when the future of the Pacific comes to be solved.

(The *Daily Telegraph*, 28 October 1908 and *The Times*, 29 October 1908)

During the War the Kaiser did something else which was tactless: he waved goodbye to some of his troops with a tennis racket.

Source 1.4

Using the Evidence

1   Why do you think some of Wilhelm's troops were upset by the way he waved goodbye to them?

2   Look at sources 1.1 and 1.2. In each case suggest which people they show. What is the artist saying about the relationship between their countries?

3   Look at source 1.4. What does it say about the Kaiser?

4   Look at the first half of source 1.3. List all the things which would have offended or worried people.

5   Wilhelm says that Germany would avoid 'complications' with a sea power like England. What do you think British people thought when they read the rest of source 1.3? How does this link with one or two of the picture sources?

2   Signing the Armistice

By the end of the War some Germans had come to resent the power of the Kaiser and those around him. Factory workers also resented the way their bosses controlled their lives. They felt that conditions might improve if they took control of the factories themselves. Many of them felt that the Kaiser should be overthrown, for he stood for everything they disliked.

Russia (the Soviet Union) was undergoing a revolution, and workers there were seizing power and deposing the wealthy ruling class, including the Tsar (the Russian Emperor). The example of Russia and the hardships and forced obedience of the wartime years convinced many Germans that the time had come for a revolution in their country, too. In the final weeks of the War (October and early November 1918) many groups of German civilians and soldiers chose soviets (councils) from among their own members. Through these soviets, the Germans

The mutineers create a 'firework' display by letting off their ammunition

The sailors' mutiny at Kiel

6

planned to run their own factories and regiments. They also planned to run the whole country by electing a 'supreme soviet'.

Some German forces began to mutiny against their commanders. This reached a climax in early November, when many German sailors refused to go into action against the British navy. They knew that the war was almost lost, and they did not want to throw their lives away pointlessly. Because of these problems the German military leaders were forced to accept defeat. British, French and German representatives travelled by train to Compiègne Forest in central France, and using their trains as offices they discussed and agreed the terms of a cease-fire (or armistice). Rear-Admiral Hope, who was one of the British representatives, wrote to his wife and told her what the meeting was like:

Source 2.1

Friday 8 November 1918
We got here about 7, and are in a siding in the middle of a beautiful forest, cut off from the world except by telephone...

[Saturday 9 November 1918]
The Boches ought to have arrived about midnight, but only got here at 7 am, in a similar train to ours, which pulled up on a siding about 100 yards [35 metres] away...

The Boches evidently wish to make it primarily a civilian affair, and the French and we are very angry with them for only sending military and naval officers of a rather subordinate rank...

They said they had come to hear the Allies' proposals for the creation of an Armistice... The terms were then read out to them and evidently made them squirm, but they were probably prepared for most of them as they must know the present military position and the state of mutiny in their fleet. When the reading of the terms was completed Winterfeldt had the cheek to ask for [an immediate] suspension of hostilities in order to save further loss of life. Of course Foch refused...

Captain Vanselow... positively cringed to us and was like a whipped dog. He said the country and army would starve if we did not remove our blockade, that their army had done very well in April and May but after that Bolshevism [Russian communism] crept in... It is remarkable that there is not a sign of the usual German arrogance and insolence from any of the party...

[Monday 11 November 1918]
The Armistice was signed at 5.15 this morning after a three hours' meeting, so that we were up all night... After signing they read a declaration saying how hard it was on the women and children and how well [the men] had fought.

(Found in P. Liddle, *Testimony of War*, Salisbury 1979)

The scene in Compiègne Forest during the Armistice negotiations

Signing the Armistice

As a result of allied blockades Germany was hit by severe food shortages and rationing was introduced. Here people queue for new ration books

The German public were shocked and resentful at the German defeat, for the War had brought them poverty and deprivation. Hunger and malnutrition were widespread, so was the grief of families where men had been crippled or killed. At the same time there was a very strong sense of relief and hope and, as we have seen, many Germans felt that the time had come to alter the way in which they were governed. However, some Germans wanted to keep the Kaiser and the traditional ways of running the country. On November 9 1918 – two days before the Armistice – the Kaiser fled to Holland to escape from the revolutionaries. His supporters hoped that he would one day be able to return to Germany, but he abdicated later that month.

_____ **Using the Evidence** _____

1   Why do you think the Armistice talks were held in a lonely place in central France?

2   Which 'Boches' does Hope name in source 2.1? Why do you think he uses this word?

3   According to Hope, how does the Germans' attitude during the armistice talks compare with their usual attitude? How does Hope seem to feel about this?

4   Who does Hope mean by 'the Allies'?
In the first half of the passage why are the Allies 'very angry'? Why should the German military leaders behave in this way?

5   How do the British and French treat the idea of having a cease-fire before the armistice is signed? Why do you think they felt like this?

6   Who does Vanselow blame for the Germans' defeat?

7   Why were Germans so short of food at the end of the War?

8   Do you think the British and their allies would have let the Kaiser stay in power? Why do you think so?

Mutineers with placards telling citizens to stay calm

3 Revolution!

The Germans' most difficult task at the end of 1918 was to salvage their pride, and German soldiers returning from France were treated like heroes:

Source 3.1 As the marchers continued into the Fatherland, it was gradually borne upon them that they were not a beaten host at all. They marched through towns and villages bedecked with flowers and flags and beneath evergreen arches erected in their honour. They were given food and boots. They were waved on their way. In Cologne such were the decorations that the marchers might have been excused for believing that they had won the war.

(F. Tuohy, *Occupied 1918–1930* London, 1931)

Source 3.2 German soldiers returning home. Notice the flags (left). People waiting to welcome returning soldiers home (below).

There is even a hint of pride in the following words by a soldier:

Source 3.3 Starving, beaten, but with our weapons, we marched back home.

(C. Zuckmayer, *A Part of Myself* London, 1970)

Many towns and cities were taken over by soldiers and sailors who had mutinied or returned from the fighting:

Source 3.4 *Lübeck, 5 November, a proclamation:* From this evening Lübeck is in our hands. Our cause is just, both at the front and at home. The corrupt military of yesterday must go, root and branch. Our aim is immediate armistice and peace. We request the people of Lübeck to remain calm. We shall do nothing to disturb the peace. Everything will be as before. We expect the populace to co-operate. We assure them that whatever changes have occurred have been made without bloodshed. We hope to continue as we have begun...

The Military Soviet

(E. Bernstein, *Die deutsche Revolution* Berlin, 1921)

Source 3.5 Hamburg, November 1918
The town was alive and full of excitement! Crowds of troops were arriving continuously from the railway stations! But they were carrying bright red bows on their rifles and red cockades on their caps. Motor lorries were surging through the streets filled with soldiers, sailors, workers. They carried red flags and posters with inscriptions: 'Long live the Revolution,' 'All Power to the Workers' and Sailors' Soviet...' Wherever we went we saw crowds of soldiers and sailors wearing red armbands... They were tearing the medals and shoulder straps from officers' uniforms.

(J. Olday, *Kingdom of Rags* London, 1939)

Source 3.6 [In Leipzig] lorries were driving up and down the street with soldiers and civilians, ... and huge red flags were waving above and behind them. Then all of a sudden an armoured car stormed through the road and men shouted: 'Clear the street! Shut the windows! Leave the balconies!' ... A second later the men in the car began to shoot into the air, into the houses, along the street... The machine-gun on the roof went off, tack-tack-tack. The shots were fired at the armoured car, but a few went astray and struck into the sandstone wall of our house, directly underneath our window and balcony. Half a dozen soldiers with rifles were just running into the house opposite. The machine-gun fired again in a battering rhythm, on and on. Then suddenly it ceased.

(L. Linke, *Restless Flags: A German Girl's Story* London, 1935)

Source 3.7 Among the marchers [in Berlin] I noticed a few soldiers who had taken off their tunics and hung them loosely over their shoulders like capes, and inside out at that. To increase the effect they had actually turned the sleeves inside out so that they hung loosely, showing their lining, like empty sausage skins..., a picturesque bit of disorderliness to show that there was now an end to war and war discipline.

(T. Wolff, *Through Two Decades*, London, 1936)

Source 3.8 Revolutionary soldiers in command

Some Berliners, led by a man called Karl Liebknecht, occupied the Kaiser's palace. Liebknecht and his followers belonged to a Communist group called the Spartacists; they supported the workers' and soldiers' soviets; they wanted Germany to adopt the Communist principles that were now being put into practice in Russia (the Soviet Union). Another group occupied the Parliament building (called the Reichstag). Their views were less extreme than those of Liebknecht and his followers, and some of them would have been willing to let the Kaiser remain as a symbol of German unity. Their main concern was that power should be in the hands of Parliament. This group formed a government with a man called Friedrich Ebert as its Chancellor (a sort of prime minister).

Ebert's government used armed force to crush a Communist rising in Berlin at the start of 1919. Hundreds of Communists were slaughtered, including their leaders Liebknecht and Rosa Luxembourg. The rising had been intended to prevent elections but these went ahead. However, the turmoil in Berlin meant that the newly-elected representatives had to meet in an opera house in Weimar instead of in the Reichstag building.

When a country is ruled by elected representatives without a king, queen or emperor it is called a republic. Germany after the First World War is sometimes known as the Weimar Republic.

A demonstration against the murders of Liebknecht and Luxembourg

A butcher's shop looted during the Revolution of 1918

Using the Evidence

1   Look at sources 3.1 and 3.2. How do they agree with each other?

2   What signs of the Germans' pride can you see in source 3.3?

3   Look at source 3.4. What group of people wrote it?

4   Look at sources 3.4, 3.5 and 3.6. How does each source show that the army was divided into men who supported the revolution and men who opposed it? Which side were most of the officers on? How can you tell? Why do you think this division existed?

5   Describe the mood in source 3.5. Why do you think the men felt like this?

6   Whose side were most civilians on? How can you tell this from source 3.5 and source 3.6?

7   Who started the trouble in source 3.6? Which side used a machine-gun? How do you think the writer felt about what she described? Why do you think so?

8   Look at sources 3.7 and 3.8. How do they both show the soldiers' attitude to war and war discipline? What attitude was it?

4   The Treaty of Versailles

German losses of land
under the Versailles Treaty

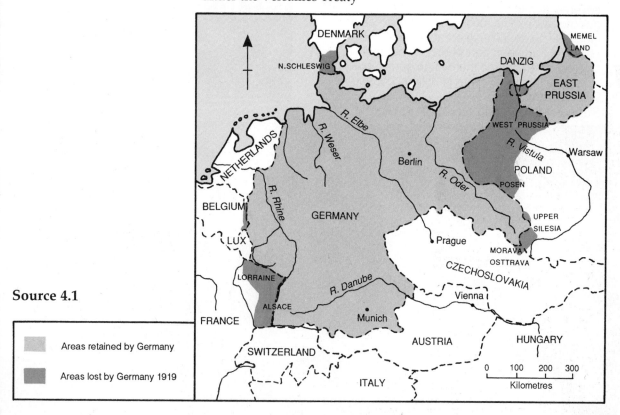

Source 4.1

Areas retained by Germany

Areas lost by Germany 1919

13

In the summer of 1919, Britain, France and their ally, America, prepared a treaty for the Germans to sign. It was called the Treaty of Versailles, and it contained the conditions on which they were willing to put a formal end to the War. Under the Treaty:

– Germany had to give up some of its territory;

– Germany had to give up its overseas colonies;

– Germany was forbidden ever to unite with its German-speaking neighbour, Austria;

– Germany had to limit its army to 100 000 men, with restrictions on their weapons and equipment;

– Germany was forbidden to station any troops to the west of the Rhine, and this area would be occupied by British, French and Belgian troops;

– Germany had to accept that it had caused the War and would have to pay the Belgians and French reparations (compensation) for the damage and loss which they had suffered.

News of the Treaty shocked the Germans severly. It was hard to accept all the blame for the War and harder still to pay for the damage, since the War had weakened the country severely and under the Treaty, France would be gaining some of its most productive mines and industrial areas. (These areas, Alsace and Lorraine, had been part of France but the Germans had gained them in an earlier war. The French felt that they were simply recovering what was theirs.)

Source 4.3   A gathering in a German city

Source 4.2   A children's street party

Some Germans felt that the Treaty was unacceptable, and some even thought of restarting the War. Von Hindenburg, commander of the field army during the War, declared, 'As a soldier I cannot help feeling that it would be better to perish honourably than accept a disgraceful peace.' Another German said, 'May the hand wither that signs this Treaty!'

With their army in ruins the Germans had little choice but to sign. They then had to set about paying the bill for reparations. The amount was staggering. It was set at 132 000 000 000 gold marks to be paid in enormous yearly instalments. German coal, ships, iron, cattle and timber would be accepted in place of some of the gold for the first few years, but it seemed that the nation would be in debt for many decades.

The following passage shows what a British writer thought about the Treaty:

Source 4.4

[The Treaty was] a piece of vengeance. It reeked with injustice. It was incapable of fulfilment. It sowed a thousand seeds from which new wars might spring... The ideals for which millions of men had fought and died – liberty, fair play, a war to end war, justice – were mocked and outraged, not by men of evil but by good men, not by foul design but with loyalty to national interests. Something blinded them...

Germany, they insisted, had to pay all the costs of the War... [It] was just as if one took the view that every German peasant, every German mother in a cheap tenement, every German worker on starvation wages, every little sempstress or university student, ten or twelve years old when the War began, shares the responsibility of those war lords and militarists who challenged the world in 1914...

The absurdity, the wild impossibility, of extracting all that vast tribute from the defeated enemy... ought to have been manifest to the most ignorant [person].

(Sir P. Gibbs, *Ten Years After*, London, 1930)

The reparations bill was huge because most of the fighting had happened in France. Germany had escaped with little damage but much of northern France lay in ruins. The following passage was written by one of the Germans who went to France to sign the Treaty:

Source 4.5

It was an overwhelming experience, even if we know from pictures and descriptions what a battlefield looks like. The greater part of the day the train was intentionally slowed down when passing through this bomb-torn, desolate country which once bore such rich fruit; past the ruins of villages and towns in which one saw almost no one, nothing but clean-up detachments at work. We crossed emergency bridges the predecessors of which were lying in the river below us. We stopped at stations between collapsed buildings, burned sheds and exploded munition trains, until we had seen all we could endure...

(A. Luckau, *The German Delegation at the Paris Peace Conference*, New York, 1941)

Using the Evidence

1 Look at source 4.1. Which countries gained territory from Germany? Which country gained most territory?
   What territories not shown on the map did Germany have to give up?

2 Which part of Germany was cut off from the rest? What did the Treaty say about Germany's relations with Austria? Compare how the Germans and their enemies

might have felt about these parts of the Treaty. Why do you think they were included?

3 Which parts of the Treaty do you think the French were most pleased about? Why?

4 Compare sources 4.2 and 4.3. One of the photographs was taken in Germany. Where do you think the other was taken? What are the children celebrating? What mood do the *Germans* seem to be in?
Suggest what news they might have heard about recently. Why do you think they have gathered together in such a way?

5 Look at source 4.4. The writer says that the Treaty 'reeked' (stank) of injustice. What injustice or injustices does he go on to mention?

6 The writer thinks that the Treaty was 'incapable of fulfilment'. Why does he think this?

7 Why do you think the train in source 4.5 was deliberately slowed down when passing through the war-torn areas?
What effect did it have on the German passengers?

Coursework

Discuss the idea that the Treaty was 'a piece of vengeance'. You could work in pairs, with one person representing the Germans and the other the French.

5   The Stab in the Back

Ebert belonged to the Social Democratic Party (the SPD), but he had formed a coalition with the Independent Socialists (the USPD). Both these socialist parties believed that major industries should be owned and run by the nation and not by wealthy individuals. In general, they disliked the power and privileges enjoyed by Germany's traditional ruling class and they wished to raise the status of the poorer people. The Independent Socialists had the more extreme views and were hated and feared by various groups in German society. Even the Social Democrats were viewed with suspicion. Ordinary soldiers (and ex-soldiers) often supported the socialist parties, but army officers, factory owners, judges and senior civil servants all opposed them. They regarded them as little better than the Communists, who aimed to abolish all class divisions. (People sometimes refer to Communists and Socialists as 'the left'

and to their opponents as 'the right'. They also speak of 'left-wing' views and 'right-wing' views. These terms come from the seating arrangement in various Parliaments. People with moderate views often sit in a central position and are known as 'the centre'.)

By 1919, some Germans had started claiming that the army had not been defeated in action but had been betrayed by socialist politicians such as Ebert. They said that the armistice of November 1918 had been a cowardly political decision by men they called the November Criminals – men who had given the army a *Dolchstoss* (a stab in the back) and had robbed the nation of victory. The government's opponents stepped up their attacks when the Treaty of Versailles was signed.

Some German soldiers had not returned to civilian life when they came home from France. They had formed unofficial brigades known as *Freikorps*. The regular army encouraged the *Freikorps*, and often let them have supplies. There were various reasons for forming the

Source 5.1

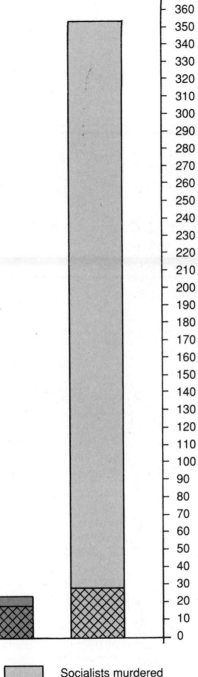

Freikorps. Some men joined because military service was the only way of life they knew. Others joined because they could not bear to think that their country had been defeated. They imagined that the *Freikorps* units might one day go into action and reverse the result of the War.

_____ **Using the Evidence** _____

1   According to the chart (source 5.1), how many socialists were murdered? How many of their opponents were murdered?

2   Which murderers usually got away with their crimes?

   Which murderers were usually caught and punished?
   What does this suggest about the police and the courts?

_____ **Coursework** _____

Design a poster or leaflet condemning the 'November Criminals'. Suggest who might have produced such a leaflet and suggest what their purpose might have been.

  Socialists murdered

  Right-wingers murdered

  No. of murders leading to convictions

Political murders in Germany from autumn 1918 to autumn 1923. (Based on data in R. Morgan (ed.) *Germany 1870–1970*, London, 1970)

6 Discontent

When it was formed, the Weimar Republic adopted a constitution (set of rules) which was meant to ensure that Germany was run more fairly than before. Under the constitution, the Reichstag had about 600 members (or deputies) who, as the Germans' elected representatives, made all the country's laws and decisions. However, there was also an elected President with powers to take action in an emergency; his most important regular task was to choose a Chancellor from among the members of the Reichstag after each election. About 25 political parties were represented in the Reichstag, but during the 1920s the Chancellor always came from the SPD, which usually had the largest number of deputies. The Chancellor's most important task was to get a number of parties to work together to form a government.

This highlights a problem which Germany faced in the 1920s. In a way, the voting system was too fair to work efficiently. Under this system, known as proportional representation, each party got the number of seats which matched its share of the total vote. Even tiny parties which attracted only a sprinkling of votes gained a handful of seats. As a result, no party had an overall majority; in other words, even the largest party could be outvoted by smaller parties acting together. The Chancellor tried to overcome this by getting a number of parties to work together as a coalition (ruling group). However, coalitions often broke down due to disagreements. When this happened a new coalition had to be formed, sometimes after a general election. Altogether, about 18 coalition governments came to power in Germany during the 1920s. All this helped to make Germany rather unstable, and it increased the desire which some people felt for a powerful ruler who did not have to bother with Parliament.

Opposition to the government

In the autumn of 1919 the government had

Source 6.1

A Freikorps member

angered the *Freikorps* by ordering them to disband. This was partly because of their lawlessness and partly because of pressure from other countries, which reminded Germany of its obligation to limit its military strength severely. No one knew the number of men in the *Freikorps* units, but it greatly exceeded what was allowed.

The *Freikorps* units were reluctant to disband, and some members claimed that Germany's fighting men were being stabbed in the back for a second time. They pointed out that the *Freikorps* units might have regained the territory which Germany had had to give to Poland. Some units stayed together by finding work on large estates in East Prussia. The sympathetic landowners there were happy to shelter the men in this way. Other units ignored the government's order as long as possible. In March 1920, one unit even held a parade. This

Source 6.2 A group of Freikorps soldiers

is how a German newspaper described the event:

Source 6.3

The Second Marine Brigade [are] crack troops that held firm against the enemy, both without and within. Steeped in patriotism, discipline, comradeship and loyalty to their leader, the brigade has given priceless, unselfish assistance to the present government in the maintenance of law and order... Today the government, now confident of survival, orders its dissolution.

The first birthday parade was held on 1 March before Their Excellencies von Luttwitz and von Throta. With band playing, banners waving, [they] filed past in perfect order. Then a field service was held under a blue sky, like the old days. Then sports and a get-together in the evening, all like the old days.

Even the weather was Hohenzollern weather. Only a single man was missing.

(*Deutsche Zeitung*, 4 March 1920)

At about this time an incident occurred in a Berlin hotel:

Source 6.4 Berlin 7 March. A scene of extraordinary violence was witnessed last night in the dining-room of the Adlon Hotel, where some of the officers of the French Mission are staying. Two of these, Captains Klein and Rougevin, were in the room at the time, the former accompanied by his wife.

Prince Joachim Albrecht of Prussia, a cousin of the ex-Kaiser and a frequent diner at the Hotel, was also present, and having observed the French officers sent word to the orchestra to play 'Deutschland über Alles' [Germany for ever]. The French officers remained sitting.

This was a signal for Prince Joachim and his party to break out into a volley of abuse and to hurl all sorts of missiles, including champagne bottles and candlesticks, at the Frenchmen. The waiters tried to protect the Frenchmen by forming a cordon around them, but without much avail. Madame Klein was assisted out by a side entrance, but one of the officers was badly maltreated and his clothes torn.

Prince Joachim has the reputation of being an extreme Pan-German and has been habitually inducing the band to play 'Deutschland über Alles', apparently with a view to provoking trouble.

(*The Times*, 7 March 1920)

Using the Evidence

1   Look at sources 6.1 and 6.2. What suggests that the Freikorps were made up of separate units?

2   Why do you think the Freikorps units and their supporters hoped to regain territory in central Europe rather than western Europe?

3   Source 6.3 says the Second Marine Brigade 'held firm against the enemy, both within and without.' In each case suggest which enemy the writer meant.

4   What government decision does the writer of source 6.3 refer to? What is his attitude to this decision?

5   Who do you think is referred to in the final sentence of source 6.3? (You may want to study the previous sentence and page 4.) What do you think this person represents for the writer?

6   A Pan-German was someone who wanted the German states to forget their differences and co-operate. What do you think Prince Joachim wanted the Germans to achieve by this?

Coursework

Pretend that you are Prince Joachim and write a brief letter to a friend in which you describe the incident in the Adlon Hotel from your own point of view.

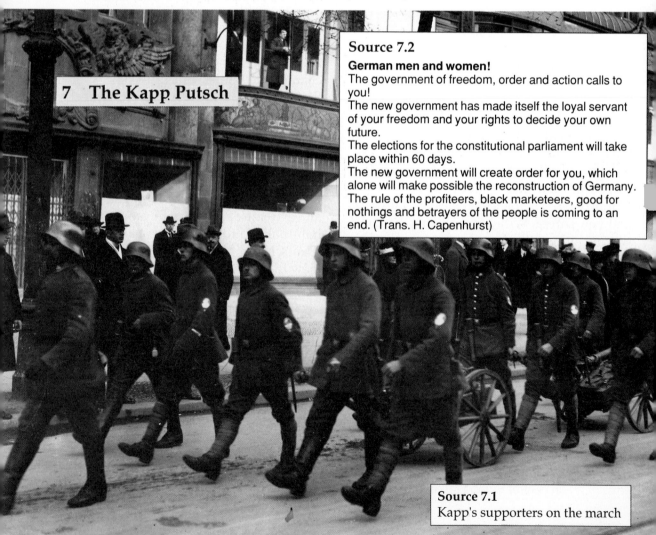

7   The Kapp Putsch

Source 7.2

German men and women!
The government of freedom, order and action calls to you!
The new government has made itself the loyal servant of your freedom and your rights to decide your own future.
The elections for the constitutional parliament will take place within 60 days.
The new government will create order for you, which alone will make possible the reconstruction of Germany. The rule of the profiteers, black marketeers, good for nothings and betrayers of the people is coming to an end. (Trans. H. Capenhurst)

Source 7.1
Kapp's supporters on the march

A politician called Gustav Kapp was pleased when he heard about the incident in the Adlon Hotel. He had founded a right-wing party called the Fatherland party and he realised that he had many supporters in and around Berlin. He therefore contacted the Commander of the Second Marine Brigade. Together they agreed that the Brigade should march on Berlin, where the Reichstag and other official buildings were now in use. They planned to overthrow Ebert's government and replace it with a government led by Kapp. The Brigade was based about 30 kilometres outside Berlin, and they marched to the city in a single night so that people would have very little chance to plan resistance. One Brigade member wrote:

Source 7.3 It was a pleasure to march that night. 2500 men on parade, 2500 men immaculate, armed to the teeth. 2500 men with but a single goal – to overthrow their own government.

(E. Junger, *Der Kampf um das Reich* (ed.) Berlin, 1937 (edited))

As the Brigade approached Berlin the government asked the official army for help, and a general called von Seekt replied:

Source 7.4 Troops do not fire on troops. You perhaps intend... that a battle be fought... between troops that have fought side by side against a common enemy? When Reichswehr [German army] fires on Reichswehr, then all comradeship within the officer corps will have vanished.

(Found in Alex de Jonge, *The Weimar Chronicle*, New York, 1978)

Ebert and several government ministers fled from Berlin, and the *Freikorps* soldiers occupied all the official buildings. However, it soon became clear that most of the city's workers were opposed to Kapp. They went on strike, and transport, water and power supplies were all cut off. Life in the city quickly broke down, and this made it very hard indeed for Kapp to run a national government.

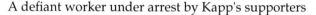

A defiant worker under arrest by Kapp's supporters

Kapp was hampered in another way too – by his own lack of planning. He seemed to have thought very little about the policies he would introduce. He pleased Berlin's students by cancelling all their examinations; and he upset the Jews who lived in the city by confiscating the flour they needed to bake bread for their Passover festival. Many Germans disliked the Jews who lived in their cities and some were pleased at what Kapp had done. However, others thought that it made him look rather mean and silly. In any case, most of his actions applied to Berlin and not to the rest of the country; Kapp was not a strong national leader.

Kapp's final problem was that the strike had prevented many local and regional newspapers from appearing. The lack of papers made it hard for Kapp to gain publicity, and many Berliners went round chanting:

All the wheels are standing still
Because it is the workers' will.

The best thing Kapp's supporters could do was hand out leaflets like the one in Source 7.2 all around the city. Despite the leaflets, few Berliners supported Kapp.

Realising that his *putsch* (or seizure of power) had failed, Kapp escaped from Berlin by flying to Sweden, and the *Freikorps* Brigade marched out of Berlin singing chants of its own. One had the words:

Why should we cry when a putsch goes wrong? There's another one coming before very long.

The soldiers were right, for the tensions in German society were increasing rapidly. Ebert's government returned to Berlin, but an army corporal called Adolf Hitler had already started to plot against it.

Source 7.5

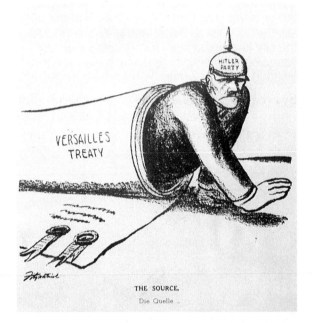

THE SOURCE.
Die Quelle

Using the Evidence

1 Look at source 7.4 and explain why General von Seekt refused to protect the government from Kapp and his followers.

2 A historian has written, 'As the man [advanced], they were greeted by Kapp, and by [a] general... in civilian dress, who just happened to be out for a walk at quarter to seven on a spring morning.' Do you think they really met by chance? Explain your opinion. What additional reason might General von Seekt have had for refusing to support the government?

3 Look at source 7.2. How does it show that wartime hardships were still being felt? What word or phrase could refer to Ebert's government?

4 What things is Kapp's leaflet (source 7.2) clear about?
   What things is it vague about? (Think carefully about the word 'reconstruction'.)
   Why should Kapp be vague about some things?

5 Explain the meaning of source 7.5.

8 Hitler's anti-Semitism

Hitler came from Austria but had volunteered for service in the German army at the start of the War. He felt, like others, that the German surrender had been a disgrace:

Source 8.1 So it had all been in vain... in vain the death of two millions. Had they died... so that a gang of criminals could lay hands on the Fatherland? I now knew that all was lost. Only fools, liars and criminals could hope for mercy from the enemy... Hatred grew within me, hatred for those responsible for the deed. Miserable and degenerate animals. My own fate now became known to me... I decided to go into politics.

(A. Hitler, *Mein Kampf*, Munich, 1925)

Hitler took his first step into politics when, soon after the War, he gained a job in the Army's Press and News Bureau. The Bureau aimed to discourage the spread of socialist and pacifist ideas among the soldiers, and Hitler was sent to spy on a tiny political party called the German Workers' Party, which was holding meetings in a cellar underneath a Munich beer hall. Hitler reported that the party was harmless and promptly joined it.

Jewish people would not have agreed that the Party – or Adolf Hitler – were harmless, for both were extremely anti-Semitic (anti-Jewish) in their views. A report Hitler wrote for his Army bosses shows some of his attitudes:

Source 8.2 There is living among us a non-German, foreign race... which nonetheless possesses all the political rights that we ourselves have. The feelings of the Jew are concerned with purely material things and his thoughts and desires even more so...

The value of the individual is no longer determined by his character, by the importance of his achievements for all, but solely by the amount of his possessions, by his money.

From this feeling emerges that concern and struggle for money and for the power to protect it which makes the Jew unscrupulous in his choice of means, ruthless in his use of them to achieve this aim...

His power is the power of money which, by attracting interest, effortlessly and interminably multiples itself in his hands. [He has] a lust for money and domination.

Anti-Semitism stemming from purely emotional reasons will always find its expression in the form of progroms [pogroms – massacres]. But anti-Semitism based on reason must lead to the systematic legal combating of the rights of the Jew... Its final aim, however, must be the uncompromising removal of the Jews altogether. Both are possible only under a government of national strength...

(16 September, 1919)

Hitler gave additional reasons for his anti-Jewish attitudes:

Source 8.3 The black-haired Jewish youth lies in wait for hours on end, gloating like a devil over the unsuspecting girl whom he plans to seduce, adulterating [contaminating] her blood and removing her from the bosom of her people.

(Found in R. Morgan, *Germany 1870–1970*, London, 1970)

Hitler also wrote of 'the nightmare vision of the seduction of thousands of girls by repulsive crooked-legged Jewish bastards'.

Hitler opposed all marriages and sexual relationships between Germans and people of other nations, including Germans of the Jewish race. He based his thinking on the idea that the Germans belonged to a superior race, called the Aryans, and must not debase their racial characteristics by inter-breeding with human beings of inferior stock. If it maintained its purity the German, or Aryan, race could one day kill or enslave all other peoples throughout the world, thus proving that it was the 'master race'.

Hitler's skills as an orator (public speaker) meant that he could whip up people's emotions at meetings. He exploited the widespread resentment felt towards wealthy Jews and encouraged people to despise all Jews because of their race. He also exploited the Germans' resentment at losing the War and their anger over the very harsh terms laid down by the winners. Under these terms, foreigners such as the British and French were treating Germany like a colony, and their military personnel were making Germans remove their hats to them when they passed in the street.

Many Jewish families had been in Germany for hundreds of years, but they, too, could be classed as 'foreign' and a few of them had made big profits during the War. The poorer Jews were overlooked since the richer ones summed up all that many Germans disliked.

Source 8.5

Hitler giving one of his speeches

In his speeches and writings Hitler tried to whip up fear of Jews as well as hatred of them. We have already seen what he said about Jewish youths corrupting German girls. He also claimed that Jews were corrupting the Germans' way of life in all sorts of hidden ways:

Source 8.4 On putting the probing knife into [a problem] I found, like a maggot in a rotting body, a little Jew, often blinded by the sudden light... Was there any shady undertaking, any form of foulness... in which at least one Jew did not participate?

(A. Hitler, *Mein Kampf*, Munich, 1925)

Source 8.6

This cartoon appeared in Germany in about 1930

Using the Evidence

1. Hitler often made sweeping statements. What generalisations did he make about Jewish people's wealth and morals?

2. Hitler misspelled the word 'pogrom' in source 8.2.
   Why might a historian be interested in a mistake like this? (In other words, what might it show about the writer?)

3. Many Jews in Germany had fled from Russia to escape from pogroms. Which of Hitler's generalisations would this make you question? Why?

4. Was Hitler worried about girls of German race or Jewish race? Why did he fear their friendships with Jews? How can you tell this from source 8.3?

5. Explain the meaning of source 8.6

6. How would Hitler like to deal with the Jews? What makes you think so?

---

9 The Nazi Manifesto

In 1920 the German Workers' Party changed its name to the National Socialist German Workers' Party (the NSDAP, or Nazi Party). It also published its manifesto (its statement of policies):

Source 9.1

1. We demand the union of all Germans in a Greater Germany.
2. We demand... the revocation of the peace treaties.
3. We demand land and territory [colonies] to feed our people and to settle our surplus population.
4. ... Only those of German blood may be members of the nation. Accordingly, no Jew may be a member of the nation.
5. Non-citizens may live in Germany only as guests and must be subject to laws for aliens.
6. All official appointments... shall be held by none but citizens...
7. ... If it should prove impossible to feed the entire population, foreign nationals [non-citizens] must be deported from the Reich [the German homeland].
8. All non-German immigration must be prevented.
9. All citizens shall have equal rights and duties.
10. It must be the first duty of every citizen to perform physical or mental work. The activities of the individual must... be for the general good.
11. We demand the abolition of incomes unearned by work [and] an end to the slavery of having to pay high interest charges.
12. ... Personal enrichment from war must be regarded as a crime against the nation. We demand, therefore, the ruthless confiscation of all war profits...
14. We demand profit-sharing in large industrial enterprises.
15. We demand the extensive development of insurance for old age.
16. We demand that... big department stores should be divided up and leased at a cheap rate to small traders, and that the utmost consideration shall be shown to all small traders in the placing of State and municipal orders.
17. We demand... the prohibition of all speculation in land.
18. We demand the ruthless prosecution of those whose activities are injurious to the common interest. Criminals, usurers [money-lenders], profiteers, etc. must be punished with death, whatever their creed or race...
20 ... The curricula of all educational establishments must be brought into line with the requirements of practical life. Schools must aim to give their pupils... a grasp of the notion of the State (through the study of civic affairs). We demand the education of gifted children of poor parents... at the expense of the State.
21. The State must ensure that the nation's health standards are raised by protecting mothers and infants, by prohibiting child labour [and] by promoting physical strength through... compulsory gymnastics and sports...
23. The publishing of papers which undermine the national welfare must be forbidden...
24. We demand freedom for all religious denominations in the State, provided they do not threaten the existence of the German race or offend its moral feelings.

25. To put... this programme into effect we demand the creation of a strong central state power for the Reich [and] the unconditional authority of the central Parliament over the entire Reich and its organisations...

(Published at an NSDAP meeting, 24 February 1920. Found in J. Noakes and G. Pridham (eds), *Documents on Nazism*, London, 1974)

A brave attempt to poke fun at the Nazis

_____ Using the Evidence _____

1   What was the Nazis' attitude to the Treaty of Versailles?

2   What would people in other European countries have thought of article (section) 3 of the manifesto?

3   Look at article 9. Do you think Jewish people would have felt reassured after reading this? Why?

4   How did articles 11 and 18 affect Jewish people?

5   Do you think the manifesto appealed to poor people or rich people most? Explain your answer.

6   Look at article 23. What do you think the Nazis would have said if someone had asked, 'But who decides what's good for the nation?'?
Point out other statements which might be queried in a similar way.

7   How do the endings of source 8.2 and source 9.1 resemble each other?

10   The SA is formed

In 1920 Hitler left the German army and in 1921 he became the leader of the Nazi party. This gave him more opportunities to speak at meetings and spread his ideas. At first, many people disagreed with Hitler's views. There were even attempts to disrupt meetings which he was addressing. This is how a Nazi newspaper called the *Veolkischer Beobachter* (the National Observer) described how the party set about crushing opposition:

Source 10.1 The NSDAP has created its own gymnastic and sports section within the framework of its organisation. It is intended to bind our young party members together to form an organisation of iron, so that it may put its strength at the disposal of the whole movement to act as a battering ram. It is intended to uphold the idea of the importance of the military for a free people. It is intended to provide protection for the propaganda activity of the leaders. But above all it is intended to develop in the hearts of our young supporters a tremendous desire for action, to drive home to them and burn into them the fact that history does not make men, but men history, and that he who allows himself to be put in the chains of slavery without any resistance deserves the yoke of slavery. It [the new section] will also encourage mutual loyalty and cheerful obedience to the leader.

The 'gymnastic and sports section' quickly came to be called the SA (the *Sturmabteilung*, or Storm-troopers). Most SA members were ex-soldiers or ex-*Freikorps* men, and the organisation had military ranks; the men wore uniform and marched in formation. They also took an oath of loyalty:

Source 10.2 As a member of the storm-troop of the NSDAP I pledge myself by its storm-flag [*sturmfahne*]: to be always ready to stake life and limb in the struggle for the aims of the movement; to give absolute military obedience to my military superiors and leaders; to bear myself honourably in and out of service; to be always companionable towards other comrades.

Despite these fine words, the SA were little better than thugs; as well as protecting Nazi meetings from disruption, they often broke up meetings conducted by other parties:

Source 10.3 The meeting, which was well attended, came to a premature end owing to an attack systematically planned by the National Socialists. National Socialist youths had early on taken seats near the speakers' platform, and numerous National Socialists were distributed as well throughout the hall. When Hitler, the leader of the National Socialists, appeared in the hall, he was greeted by his followers with demonstrative applause... and they occupied the platform. But a large section of the meeting protested and demanded that Ballerstedt [the leader of the Bavarian League] should speak. He had pushed his way through to the platform, but he could not begin because the National Socialists were all the time shouting 'Hitler!' The uproar grew even worse when someone tried to prevent the fight that was feared by switching off the electricity. When the lights came on again, Ballerstedt declared that

anybody who tried to disturb the meeting would be charged with disturbing the peace. After this the young people on the platform, many of them barely in their teens, surrounded him, beat him up and pushed him down the platform steps. Ballerstedt received a head injury which bled badly. As the audience were naturally growing more and more excited... a fairly strong group of state police then cleared the hall.

(From a report in the *Münchner Neueste Nachrichten*)

Source 10.4

The SA 'Brownshirt' uniform

1   Why do you think the SA was started as a 'gymnastics and sports' section?

2   What clues can you see in source 10.1 that the SA was a military organisation?

3   What do you think the writer thought of the new organisation? Why do you think so?

4   What 'slavery' might the writer of source 10.1 have meant?

5   What details in source 10.3 suggest that the Nazis had planned in advance to disrupt Ballerstedt's meeting?

6   What do you think Ballerstedt felt about the way in which the police had acted? Why?

11   Passive Resistance and Hyper-inflation

In January 1923 the following reports appeared in *The Times*:

Source 11.1 [10 January] The French government have decided to proceed to the occupation of the Ruhr area [a border region of Germany]... The immediate occasion for the march into the Ruhr is the resolution adopted by the Reparations Commission yesterday declaring Germany in voluntary default in respect of coal deliveries...

The French are going to work in the Ruhr with a considerable display of military force. Engineers are being sent to determine the capacity of mines and to collect certain dues from the highly-organised production of the Ruhr... At the moment, however, it is the military aspect of the movement that is most obvious. Our Correspondent in the Ruhr vividly describes the gathering of troops in field-kit... and all the eager turmoil that precedes an advance... It is evident that the French are taking no risks and, whatever the functions of their engineers may be, they will be carefully guarded...

The French idea is to exert pressure upon the big German industrialists... whose activities are centred in the Ruhr and who are, in fact, the pillars of the German industrial system. Many of the industrialists have undoubtedly been profiting as a result of the... general disorganisation of German finance...

The German people, whose lot is far from easy now, will be plunged by the separate action of France into a state of still more... acute suffering. [This] cannot promote the establishment of true peace in Europe, and on the other hand it constitutes a strong temptation to those forces of social disorder which are now the only real danger...

Source 11.2 [12 January] At 20 minutes to 2 [on January 11] the main body of the French forces came down the hill leading... to the railway station and chief post office [in Essen, a city in the Ruhr]. At the head rode a party of cyclists in dark blue uniform and steel helmets, closely followed by five... armoured cars. From these grim-looking cars, of which the occupants were invisible, stood out the muzzles of machine-guns, a silent threat to the sullen crowd.

Many took no trouble to hide the hatred in their hearts. Near the station I saw a man of some 30 years suddenly turn aside with a sob and mutter, 'The swine. My God, the pack of swine. May God pay them out for this cruel outrage.' ... Everyone's face was set in the effort to preserve his control or had already lost it in some cry of fury or pain...

The French looked straight before them, sparing no glance for the... angry men... They halted before the door of the Council Chamber... 'General Rampon, commanding the French troops who are occupying Essen, requests the presence of [the Mayor].'
'I am [his deputy],' was the reply.
'Then you will please [come here]?'
'Pardon, Monsieur – I can only receive official visits.

Source 11.3   A consignment of coal

Source 11.4 [January 12] The idea of using the existing German industrial organisation in the Ruhr as a means of diverting to French use a percentage of the coal production has been partly frustrated by the removal to Hamburg of the personnel and the archives of the Coal Syndicate, which was the crown of the intricate organisation of the Ruhr industry... The removal of this central body and the department of mining officials will make it necessary for the French themselves to take over... the management of the mines and to remodel the industrial administration of the district... Already military occupation is overshadowing economic occupation and may render the execution of the scheme more difficult. It is not easy to dig coal with bayonets.

The Germans in the Ruhr went on strike, and they did whatever they could to stop the French invaders from running their industries. They carried out acts of sabotage, and several factories were set on fire. Mines became flooded and heavy machinery fell to pieces because of a sudden lack of bolts!
    The Germans' defiant action meant that the French gained nothing from what they had done. Instead of increasing, supplies of goods from the Ruhr fell sharply. One man wrote:

Source 11.5 At Gedesberg I noticed a truck which had been loaded with sacks of corn on the day the French first seized the line... The corn had sprouted merrily and now stood a foot and a half [half a metre] high.

The Germans were suffering far more severely than the French. The Ruhr had Germany's most productive mines and factories and the shutdown was ruining Germany's already weak economy. In the autumn of 1923 the Germans promised to send reparations on time in future and the French withdrew their forces. Production in the Ruhr resumed but by this time the German economy was in total chaos.
    The most serious problems were those affecting the German currency. The value of the mark had already been falling. The process had started during the War, when the German government had printed extra bank-notes in order to pay for armaments. It continued as the Germans printed money to pay reparations. By

the time the French marched into the Ruhr 250 marks were needed to buy a loaf of bread which had cost half a mark only five years earlier. The rise in prices gathered pace at a frightening rate; by the autumn of 1923 a loaf cost 200 000 000 000 marks.

Unlike money, a thing like a basket kept its value. Traders accepted all sorts of items in place of cash, and Germans began to barter goods like primitive tribespeople.

Poverty grew extremely severe, for although wages rose they did not keep up with the rise in prices, and many people had nothing left in their homes they could barter. Food was scarce and people in queues often watched in despair as price tags were changed. Posting letters became difficult because there was insufficient room on an envelope for all the stamps that were needed. Husbands who worked away from home knew that posting parcels of money to their families was useless; the money would lose nearly all its value before it reached them.

Source 11.6
A chest full of almost worthless money

Source 11.7
A street scene when things were at their worst

The poor could do little to ease the effects of this hyper-inflation (rapid fall in the value of money). It is said that they sometimes economised by papering their walls with bank-notes, since this was cheaper than buying wallpaper. Pillows and quilts could be made by stuffing bank-notes into suitable bags, and money was sometimes burned as a cheap way of keeping warm.

People who had spent their lives in lodgings saving hard for a home of their own saw the value of their savings disappear. At the start of 1923 a couple might have been nearly ready to buy a house; by the end of the year they might have been able to buy a pile of bricks or a doorknob.

The Germans noticed that a few groups of people in Germany seemed to be doing quite well. These groups included foreigners such as the British and French, for a little of their currency bought them billions of marks each day. A writer called Alex de Jonge makes this clear. He tells the story of an Englishman who called at a money-changing office during a visit to the Ruhr. 'He produced a pound note and the dealer was so overcome by such wealth that he waved his hand at his stock of currency and invited the Englishman to help himself.' The following passage was written by another Englishman:

Source 11.8 You could have any food you wanted if you could pay for it... I used to go to the Königshalle (that was the big café in Bonn) ... for... a large piece of toast with fresh shrimps and mayonnaise. For a German that would have been quite impossible.

I paid two million marks for a glass of beer. You changed as little money as you could every day. No, one did not feel guilty, one felt it was perfectly normal, a gift from the gods. Of course there was hatred in the air, and I dare say a lot of resentment against foreigners, but we never noticed it. They were still beaten you see, a bit under and occupied.

(A. Swan quoted by A. de Jonge in *The Weimar Chronicle*, New York. 1978)

A demonstration against the French in the Ruhr

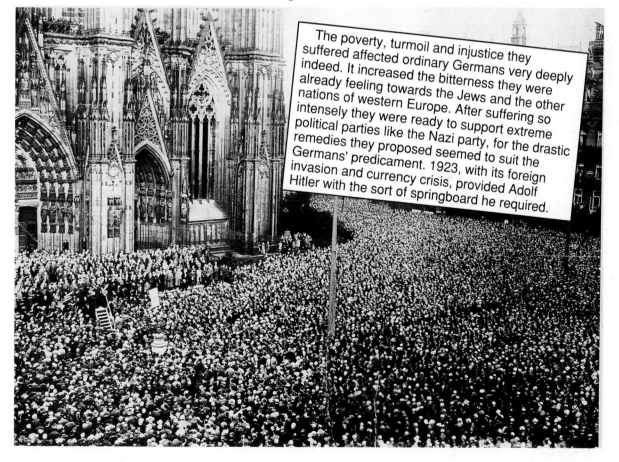

The poverty, turmoil and injustice they suffered affected ordinary Germans very deeply indeed. It increased the bitterness they were already feeling towards the Jews and the other nations of western Europe. After suffering so intensely they were ready to support extreme political parties like the Nazi party, for the drastic remedies they proposed seemed to suit the Germans' predicament. 1923, with its foreign invasion and currency crisis, provided Adolf Hitler with the sort of springboard he required.

1 What did the French do in Germany in 1923 and why did they do it?

2 According to *The Times*, what problem or problems did they encounter?

3 What point was the German making in Source 11.2 when he said, 'I can only receive official visits'? What do you think might have happened to him after this?

4 What fears and concerns did *The Times* have about what the French were doing?

5 Look at source 11.5 and suggest what the man in source 11.3 is doing.

6 Why do you think the writer of source 11.8 changed as little money as he could each day?

7 Look at source 11.7. What do you think the women are doing?

8 Think about the clues in this section and then try to answer the following questions:
   a) Why did Germans rush to the shops as soon as they had any money?
   b) Why did they sometimes have to carry their money in baskets instead of purses or wallets?
   c) Why did thieves sometimes snatch people's baskets and tip out the money as they ran away?
   d) How did wealthy people gain by paying debts late but getting payments as quickly as possible?
   e) How would hyper-inflation affect someone (such as a builder) who agreed a price for a certain job before he began it?

---

12 Hitler's Putsch

One of the weaknesses of the Weimar constitution was that it gave the lander a great deal of power, and this undermined the authority of the Berlin government. To make matters worse, the division of power between the central and state authorities was rather unclear, causing frequent disputes. People who felt that the Germans had been betrayed to their enemies often supported the lander against the Berlin government.

In the state of Bavaria there was an organisation called the *Kampfbund*, which linked the SA and other illegal armed groups. Hitler lived in Bavaria and he wanted *Kampfbund* forces to march on Berlin and overthrow the central government. He hoped that a new national government would then be founded in Munich, Bavaria's capital, and he wanted this new government to unify Germany and lead it against its enemies.

The *Kampfbund* had enormous influence in Bavaria. The state was run by a man called Kahr, who sympathised with Hitler's aims.

However, Kahr believed that 'An agreed, well-prepared and well-thought-out plan must be followed,' while Hitler wished to act at once. One reason for Hitler's haste was the fact that the Berlin government was solving the problems of the Ruhr and Germany's currency. The German public might never forgive the government for what had happened; even so, their panic and despair was sure to diminish, and this would reduce their support for extremists such as Hitler.

Hitler decided to start a rising and make Kahr support it. On 8 November, 1923, Kahr was addressing a political meeting at a Munich beer hall, and Hitler surrounded the building with 600 SA men. A witness who was in the hall describes what followed:

Source 12.1 I saw [Hitler] appear between two armed soldiers in steel helmets who carried pistols next to their heads, pointing at the ceiling... Hitler made a sign to the man on his right, who fired a shot at the ceiling. Thereupon Hitler called out (I cannot remember the exact order of his words) 'The national revolution has broken out. The hall is surrounded.' Maybe he mentioned the exact number, I am not sure. He asked Kahr, Lossow [the Bavarian army commander] and Seisser [the Bavarian police chief] to come out, and he guaranteed their personal freedom. The gentlemen did not move. [Kahr] had stepped back and stood opposite Hitler, looking at him calmly. Then Hitler went towards the platform. What happened I could not see exactly. I heard him talk to the gentlemen and I heard the words: Everything would be over in ten minutes if the gentlemen would go out with him. To my surprise the three gentlemen went out with him immediately...

Hitler re-entered about ten minutes later... When he stepped onto the platform the disturbance was so great that he could not be heard, and he fired a shot... When things did not become quiet he shouted angrily at the audience: 'If you are not quiet I shall have a machine-gun put in the gallery.' In fact he had come to say that his prediction of everything being over in ten minutes had not come true. But he said it in such a way that he finally went out with the permission of the audience to say to Kahr that the whole assembly would be behind him if he were to join. It was a complete reversal. One could hear it being said that the whole thing had been arranged, that it was a phoney performance. I did not share this opinion because Kahr's attitude seemed to contradict it. Seeing him at close quarters, one got the impression of confusion, of great dismay...

(E. Deuerlein, *Der Hitler-Putsch...*, Stuttgart, 1962)

The following police report continues the story:

Source 12.2 Hitler returned [to the side room], this time without a pistol. He talked about his second speech in the hall and the jubilation it had produced, and he pressed the gentlemen further. Suddenly... Ludendorff [a famous general] entered the room in a hat and coat and, without asking any questions, with obvious excitement and with a trembling voice, declared: 'Gentlemen, I am just as surprised as you are. But the step has been taken, it is a question of the Fatherland and the great national and racial cause, and I can only advise you, go with us and do the same.'

... After long urging, Kahr declared: 'I am ready to take over the destiny of Bavaria as the representative of the monarchy.'

The witness in the hall describes what happened next:

Source 12.3 An hour after Hitler's first appearance the three gentlemen came back into the hall with Hitler and Ludendorff. They were enthusiastically received. On the platform Kahr began to speak first and gave the speech which was printed word for word in the papers. Ludendorff, too, in my opinion spoke without being requested to, whereas Lossow and Seisser only spoke after repeated requests – I can't remember the words, but only the gestures – on Hitler's part...

Kahr's face was like a mask all evening. He was not pale or agitated; he was very serious, but spoke very composedly... Hitler, on the other hand, ... was radiant with joy... a kind of childlike joy...

Using the Evidence

1 *Briefly* summarise the main events in the beer hall on 8 November, 1923.

2 In source 12.1 the witness says, 'I cannot remember the exact order of [Hitler's] words.' What similar remarks does he make in sources 12.1 and 12.3? Do these remarks make him seem a reliable witness or an unreliable one? (It may be worth discussing this.)

3 List the different things the witness says about Kahr's appearance. Do they contradict each other? How does this affect your opinion of the witness?

4 Near the end of source 12.1 the witness mentions the idea that 'the whole thing... was a phoney performance.' What performance is he referring to? Why might Kahr and the others have put on an act?

5 Do you think Ludendorff was really surprised at what was happening? Give one or two reasons for your view.

6 In this incident what different ways did Hitler have of getting people to do what he wanted?

---

13   Hitler's Trial and Fortress Arrest

It seemed that Hitler's putsch was succeeding. However, by the following day Kahr, Lossow and Seisser had withdrawn their support. In spite of this setback, Hitler decided to go ahead with a march through the centre of Munich. It soon became clear that Seisser had ordered the police to stop them:

Source 13.1 Numerous civilians hurried on ahead of the actual column... and pushed the police barricade. The ceaseless shouts of 'Stop! Don't go on!' by the state police were not obeyed... They were received with fixed bayonets, guns with the safety catches off, and raised pistols. Several police officers were spat upon, and pistols with the safety catches off were stuck in their chests. The police used rubber truncheons and rifle butts and tried to push back the crowd with rifles held horizontally...

Suddenly a National Socialist fired a pistol at a police officer from close quarters. The shot went past his head and killed Sergeant Hollweg standing behind him. Even before it was possible to give an order, [his] comrades opened fire as the Hitler lot did, and a short gun battle ensued during which the police were also shot at from the Preysingpalais and from the house which contained the Café Rottenhöfer. After no more than 30 seconds the Hitler lot fled...

(An official report quoted in Deuerlein, *Der Hitler-Putsch...*)

On 26 February 1924, Hitler, Ludendorff and other conspirators were put on trial for treason, and Kahr, Lossow and Seisser gave evidence against them. Hitler used the trial as a chance to make stirring political speeches, and he stood up for what he and Ludendorff had done at the beer hall:

Source 13.2 We wanted to create in Germany the conditions which will make it possible for the iron grip of our enemies to be removed from us. We wanted to... take up the fight... for the duty of bearing arms – of military service. And now I ask you: Is that high reason?

A modern writer has described the trial as a 'farce':

Source 13.3
It was a trial in name only, in reality an anti-republican celebration... When Ludendorff appeared in court the army guard presented arms and the entire court rose to its feet. Because he had prudently worn civilian dress during the putsch he was pronounced innocent. (Indeed, one ex-Nazi has maintained that had he worn uniform the putsch would have succeeded.) When he drove away his car was covered with flowers, surrounded by cheering crowds and had a Swastika on the hood. He was to remain head of all paramilitary organisations, 'the supreme head of the secret Reichswehr.'

Hitler and some of his friends during Hitler's fortress arrest

... The sentence passed on Hitler was a disaster. He was given four years' *Festungshaft*, fortress arrest. This was less a prison sentence than a compliment... [It] was a sentence reserved for 'naughty boys' of good family – students or officers who had killed their man in a duel. It was taken as a joke and a compliment. Tales were told of students under fortress arrest borrowing money from their jailors to spend a weekend in Berlin... It was his association with Ludendorff that earned Hitler... this most harmless... of sentences, which conferred a monstrous prestige upon him. No wonder his guards in Festung Landsberg used to [greet] him with his own *Hitler Gruss* [his special salute]!

(A. de Jonge, *The Weimar Chronicle*)

In prison Hitler put his political views into writing. He was released from prison after only five months, but by that time his famous book *Mein Kampf (My Struggle)* was almost complete.

Using the Evidence

1 Some people think that Kahr, Lossow and Seisser had planned the 'beer cellar putsch' with Hitler. What do you think? Try to give reasons, using evidence from this chapter and the previous one.

2 What attitude does the writer of source 13.1 have to Hitler's supporters? How can you tell?

3 Who seem most to blame for the violence and shooting in source 13.1 – the civilians or the police? How does the source give you this idea?

4 Do you have enough evidence to be *sure* who caused the violence and shooting? Whose side of the story seems to be missing?

5 How was Ludendorff's choice of clothes important?

6 Someone has said that 'the only successful aspect of Hitler's putsch was his trial.' What do you think he meant by this?

7 What main aims did Ludendorff and Hitler have when they tried to seize power? (Use sources 12.2 and 13.2, as well as things you already know.)

_____ **Coursework** _____

Someone has said, 'History is always written by the winners.' Why might this be and what are the dangers?

14   'We Must Have Power!'

At the time of Hitler's 'beer cellar putsch' a man called Gustav Stresemann had been the German Chancellor. Stresemann had made himself unpopular by ending passive resistance in the Ruhr and resuming the payment of reparations. However, Stresemann felt that Germany needed better relations with other countries; instead of defying them Germany ought to win their trust. He argued that this was the only way to get better treatment – and more independence. He secretly hoped that Germany might then regain its old strength and win back some of the territories which it had lost.

At the end of 1923 Stresemann resigned as Chancellor and became Foreign Minister. He continued his policy of improving Germany's relations with the rest of the world. One of his first achievements was to reach an agreement known as the Dawes Plan. Under the Plan, reparations instalments were greatly reduced and American banks agreed to lend Germany large sums of money.

The collapse of the mark had left many German industries without any money for new investment; the Dawes Plan provided this much-needed cash. New factories could now be built and new machines could be installed. This, in turn, provided the Germans with more employment and extra cash with which to buy goods such as cars and radios.

Germany seemed to be entering a period of stability and prosperity. As Hitler had feared, resentment against the government was fading away and people were not prepared to elect extreme political parties such as the Nazis or the Communists. In spite of this, the failure of Hitler's putsch had taught him to seek power legally, through elections. Only after gaining power would he set himself above the law and become a dictator. These attitudes are clear from things which Hitler wrote in his book *Mein Kampf*:

Source 14.1 For us [Nazis], Parliament is not an end, but a means to an end. We are a parliamentary party by necessity and are forced to be so by the constitution. We do not fight for seats in Parliament for their own sake, but for the day when we can liberate the German nation.

Source 14.2 In small things and in great the [Nazi] movement stands for the unquestioned authority of the Leader. The National State must work to set all governments free from the control of majorities. Decisions shall be made by one man.

In the following source a man called Otto Strasser emphasises Hitler's determination to see the Nazis (and himself) in power:

Source 14.3 I remember one of my first conversations with him. It was really our first quarrel.

'Power,' screamed Adolf. 'We must have power.'

'Before we gain it,' I replied firmly, 'Let us decide what we propose to do with it...'

Hitler, who even then could hardly bear contradiction, thumped on the table and barked: 'Power first! Afterwards we can act as circumstances dictate.'

(Otto Strasser, *Hitler and I,* London, 1940)

Source 14.4 'Only the stupidest calves choose their own butchers'

Using the Evidence

1 Explain what Hitler meant when he said, 'Power is not an end but a means to an end.' What form of government was Hitler aiming to introduce?

2 The Nazi Party had issued a manifesto (see source 9.1). Why was this of little value in showing what the Nazis would do if they gained power?

3 Suggest one or two advantages and disadvantages in a system where decisions are made by one person. Why might such a system have appealed to Germans in the time of the Weimar Republic?

4 Look at source 14.4 and try to explain what the artist is saying.

In 1922 a man called Benito Mussolini seized power in Italy and began to rule as a dictator. The frequent changes of government in Germany led some Germans to wish for a dictator in their country too. This became clear in 1924, when the Nazis stood for election for the first time and gained 32 seats. However, in the next election (held seven months later) the number of Nazi seats fell to 14. It seemed that Stresemann's policies were bringing contentment.

One of Stresemann's greatest achievements was to make a Treaty with Germany's former enemies in western Europe. The Treaty was signed in 1925 at Locarno in Switzerland and is called the Treaty of Locarno. The Treaty bound Belgium, France and Germany to honour their existing boundaries, and this reduced fears that the Germans might try to regain the border provinces of Alsace and Lorraine. Trust was increased and Britain and France agreed to reduce their forces in Germany.

At last, in 1926, Germany joined the League of Nations. The League had been formed in 1919, with over 60 countries as members. Their representatives met at Geneva in Switzerland to discuss international problems and solve them peacefully. At first they would not allow the Germans and their allies in the First World War to join the League, and some people said that the League was simply a club for the winners. When they finally let the Germans join it seemed that Germany had been accepted by the family of nations.

Stresemann continued to raise his country's prosperity, and in 1929 he reached a new agreement with American financiers. Under this scheme, which was known as the Young Plan, loans from American banks were increased and the arrangements for paying reparations were made even easier.

The Dawes Plan and the Young Plan ensured that the Germans had money with which to pay reparations. France and Belgium depended on the reparations to pay back war loans received from Great Britain, and Britain used the money to pay back war loans received from America. All this meant that money was going round and round from country to country.

The cycle worked smoothly for most of the 1920s. However, it was rather a risky arrangement, for a single problem at any stage could cause the cycle to break down completely. This eventually happened, as we shall see, and it caused a crisis which affected many parts of the world. However, things went well in the late 1920s; Germany, America and other countries seemed to be thriving and trust between them continued to grow. At last, in 1929, foreign troops were withdrawn from the Rhineland. The Germans still had to pay reparations and many of them resented this, but their bitterness was slowly diminishing. Even so, the threat of unrest and military conflict had not disappeared. Germany's forces were stronger than many people thought, for they had been re-arming secretly. There seemed little hope of regaining land in western Europe but many officers hoped to win back the territories lost to Poland, Czechoslovakia and Lithuania. Hitler agreed with this idea:

Source 15.1 We National Socialists must... secure for the German people the land and soil to which they are entitled on this earth...

State boundaries are made by man and changed by man... No little nigger nation or other is involved but Germany, which has given the present-day world its culture.

We... draw a line beneath the foreign policy of our pre-War period... We stop the endless German movement to the south and west and turn our gaze towards the lands in the east... If we speak of soil in Europe today our main thoughts must be of Russia and the servant states on her border...

(Mein Kampf)

Hitler has spent the late 1920s giving speeches and watching out for a chance to gain power. He seemed to be winning very little support. When Stresemann died on 3 October 1929, Germany had increasing debts but thriving factories, satisfied voters and international recognition. However, things were soon to change, for a few weeks later the world's finances were thrown into chaos, and this gave Hitler the chance that he had been waiting for.

Source 15.2 A 'money cycle' which operated during the 1920s

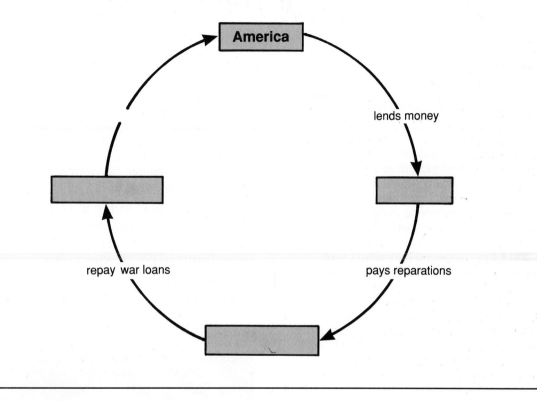

Using the Evidence

1   Study source 15.1. What attitude does Hitler have to Germany? What attitude does he have to other nations? How can you tell?

2   Which nations might have felt safer after reading source 15.1? Which nations might have felt more at risk? In each case say why.

3   Was Hitler content with getting back the lands which Germany had lost? Explain your answer.

Coursework

Copy the diagram (Source 15.2) and fill in the blank spaces. Explain the risks which such a cycle of money involved.

---

3 Rise of the Nazis

16 The Wall Street Crash

On 29 October 1929 the value of shares in American companies suddenly slumped. This is known as the Wall Street Crash (after Wall Street, New York, where American brokers traded in shares). The Crash had many causes. One was the very high price of shares. People with shares hoped to sell them at a profit; however, they knew that prices could fall at any time, and if this happened they would lose money. In October 1929 nervousness over this increased. People hurried to sell their shares, and the nervousness grew even worse. At last, on 29 October, the shareholders panicked; they flooded the market with millions of shares which no one would buy, and as a result the prices plunged.

Some people had bought their shares with loans. They had planned to pay back the loans when they sold the shares at a profit. However, the Crash left them penniless and deeply in debt. Many had to sell their homes and live on the streets or in shanty towns. The ruin spread throughout America, for companies found that fewer people could afford to buy the goods they were making. They cut production, and this meant sacking millions of workers. The jobless workers were also very short of money, so sales and production fell again and more workers were sacked.

Many individuals and companies failed to pay back loans they had taken from banks, and the banks began to suffer, too. They therefore, demanded the prompt repayment of loans they had made to foreign customers, including German companies. Paying the money back at short notice ruined a lot of these companies, and recession and unemployment therefore spread to Germany. It also spread to other countries, for money cycles like the one described in chapter 15 were broken. Trade between nations slumped as the ruin spread round the world, and this made conditions even worse.

At the time of the Wall Street Crash only 1 400 000 Germans were unemployed. Within two years the figure had risen to over 6 000 000.

Hunger and despair were widespread, and people had to scavenge for food as they had done ten years earlier. Few people starved but only the wealthy avoided hardship and deprivation.

Hitler was glad that the Germans were suffering so severely:

Source 16.1 Never in my life have I been so well disposed and inwardly contented as in these days. For hard reality has opened the eyes of millions of Germans to the... swindles, lies and betrayals of the Marxist [Communist] deceivers of the people.

Source 16.2

A political poster

The Communist Party was just one of the many political parties in Germany at this time. Hitler picked on the Communists for various reasons:

– They had been among the leading rebels at the end of the First World War, and Hitler felt that they shared the blame for Germany's defeat;

- They supported Russia, and Hitler hoped that the Germans might one day expand into Russia;

- They believed in everything being shared, including workshops and factories. By contrast, the Nazis favoured private businesses, and Hitler wanted good relations with factory owners, who might donate to Nazi funds;

- The Communists believed in running things through soviets, while Hitler's aim was to be the Germans' *Führer* (Leader) with as much power as possible for himself.

The revolution in Russia had brought the Communists to power there after the First World War. Many wealthy and influential people in western Europe feared that the Communist system would spread, and some of them therefore supported Hitler.

Using the Evidence

1 In source 16.1 who does Hitler mean by 'the Marxist deceivers of the people'? Which political parties is he lumping together? Why do you think he is doing this?

2 Why do you think he was pleased that people's 'eyes had been opened'?

3 Study source 16.2. What do you think the artist was saying? Who do you think put the poster up? Why do you think so?

4 Compare source 16.2 with source 8.6. What stereotypes (fixed ideas) about Jewish people do they encourage?

5. In your opinion, what are the dangers in thinking of people as types and not as individuals?

17   Threats to Democracy

Democracy is decision-making by the public (normally through elected representatives). By 1930 the Germans had lost faith in their democratic system, and fighting was breaking out on the streets of the larger cities. It seemed that many Germans saw a civil war as the only way to settle their differences. The Communists and Nazis had always opposed each other, and groups of them often paraded and fought in city streets:

Source 17.1 Bodies of both Communists and Nazis were to be seen every weekend, parading in uniform, with a band at their head. They frequently came to blows. I wondered at first how they contrived to distinguish their enemies from their friends in those fracas, for their uniforms were remarkably similar... On closer investigation I found the Nazis were mostly of middle-class origin, and the Communists nearly all working-class youths. But as regards outward appearance there was little to choose between them.

(B. Reynolds, *Prelude to Hitler*, London, 1933)

Source 17.2

ELECTIONS FOR THE REICHSTAG

	Party	May 1928	Sept 1930
Left-wing parties	Communist	54	77
	Social Democratic	152	143
	Independent Socialist	-	-
	Bavarian People's	17	19
	Hanoverian	3	3
Centre parties	Catholic Centre	61	68
	People's	45	30
	Democrat	25	14
	Economic	23	23
	Independents	-	51
Right-wing parties	Nationalist	79	41
	National Socialist	12	107
	Total Seats	471	576

Shortly before elections were held in 1930 some German states banned the wearing of SA and similar uniforms in the hope that this would reduce the street violence. The Nazis simply

A Nazi parade

made fun of this by parading in white shirts (instead of brown) and by wearing bottle tops instead of badges. After the elections, the new Nazi members of the Reichstag put on brown shirts when they entered the building. Their entry was accompanied by attacks on Jewish property throughout Berlin, as Nazi supporters celebrated their Party's success. Like the new Nazi members of the Reichstag, they were showing their defiance of Germany's laws and the bodies which made them.

A further stage in the breakdown of law and democracy came when the Chancellor, Heinrich Brüning, asked von Hindenburg to dissolve the Reichstag and let him rule with the help of a group of ministers. The Weimar constitution permitted this to be done in an emergency, and Brüning ruled in this way throughout 1931. Although it was legal it prepared the way for a Nazi dictatorship (rule by one man with unlimited authority).

Brüning and Hindenburg were able to justify what they did by pointing out that Hindenburg had been elected. They could therefore claim that his actions had the people's support.

Using the Evidence

1   Why do you think the Communist and Nazi groups liked parading with bands and uniforms?

2   Why do you think Nazis stood for election and took seats in the Reichstag if they had no respect for the Reichstag and the laws it made?

3   Brüning belonged to the Roman Catholic Centre Party, and the left-wing and right-wing parties opposed his coalitions with other parties. Look at source 17.2 and suggest why Brüning had the Reichstag dissolved after the 1930 elections.

In the spring of 1932, Hitler stood against Hindenburg in the German presidential election. Hindenburg won but only narrowly. The Nazi threat was stronger than ever. This became clear when Brüning fell from power in the summer. Brüning's successor, Count von Papen, needed to form a coalition, and general elections were therefore held. The elections showed a surge of support for the Nazi Party. They gained 230 seats, thus becoming the largest part in the Reichstag. They still had less than half the seats, and this meant that other parties could combine to outvote them. It also meant that Hitler did not have a right to become the Chancellor, but he went to President Hindenburg and asked to be appointed:

Part of the 'Ten years' celebration

Source 18.1 Hindenburg replied that because of the tense situation he could not in good conscience risk transferring the power of government to a new party such as the National Socialists, which did not command a majority and which was intolerant, noisy and undisciplined.

At this point, Hindenburg, with a certain show of excitement, referred to several recent occurrences – clashes between the Nazis and the police, acts of violence committed by Hitler's followers against those who were of different opinions, excesses against Jews and other illegal acts. All these incidents had strengthened him in his conviction that there were numerous wild elements in the Party beyond control... After extended discussion Hindenburg proposed to Hitler that he should declare himself ready to co-operate with the other parties... and that he should give up the one-sided idea that he must have complete power... [He also mentioned] the widespread fear that a National Socialist government would make ill use of its power and would suppress all other viewpoints and gradually eliminate them...

Hitler was adamant, however, in refusing to put himself in the position of bargaining with the leaders of the other parties...

(*Nazi Conspiracy and Aggression*, Washington, 1946, quoted in W. Shirer, *The Rise and Fall of the Third Reich*, London, 1960)

Source 18.2 The discussion [above] was followed by a short conversation in the corridor... in which Herr Hitler expressed the view that future developments would lead to... the overthrow of the Reich President. The Government would get into a difficult position; the opposition would become very sharp and he could assume no responsibility for the consequences.

(From a minute of Hitler's meeting with the President by O. Meissner)

Source 18.3

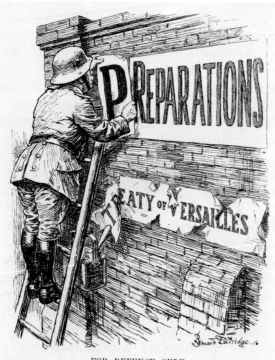

FOR DEFENCE ONLY.
GERMANY. "I NEVER DID LIKE THE LOOK OF THAT OLD WORD."

1   Why might Germans have been discontented with the form of democracy they had under Brüning? How might voting for the Nazi Party have been a way of expressing their feelings?

2   Hindenburg said that the Nazi Party was 'intolerant'. How did he repeat or emphasise this in source 18.1?

3   What was Hitler's attitude after his discussion with Hindenburg? Suggest how he might have answered some of Hindenburg's points.

4   Look at source 18.3, which appeared in Britain while Hitler was campaigning for the Chancellorship. Explain what it means and say what it shows about British feelings.

This ominous cartoon appeared in the British magazine *Punch* in 1932

---

19   Hitler's Triumph

In spite of Hitler's anger and threats a man called Sleicher took over from Papen. However, he only held office for 57 days, and in January 1933 Hindenburg had to choose another new Chancellor. This time the Nazis may have put unfair pressure on him to make him choose Hitler. Otto von Meissner, one of Hindenburg's secretaries, wrote of a secret meeting between Hitler and Oskar von Hindenburg, the President's son. After the meeting, which was held at the home of a leading Nazi supporter, 'Oskar was very silent; the only remark he made was that there was no help for it: the Nazis had to be taken into the government.' Some people think that the Hindenburgs had plotted a tax fraud and Hitler had threatened to publish the details in a Nazi paper.

Hitler still had a genuine claim to the Chancellorship, since the Nazis remained the largest party in the Reichstag. Papen, who was a friend of Hindenburg, advised him that only a Nazi could command sufficient support to stay in power. He paid several visits to Hindenburg to discuss the matter, and in the end they agreed that Hitler should be appointed – but only on certain strict conditions.

Hindenburg acted accordingly. On 30 January 1933 he called Hitler to his palace and appointed him to the Chancellorship but insisted on making Papen vice-Chancellor. Papen's views were less extreme than Hitler's and would help to ensure a proper balance. He also insisted on having no more than two or three Nazis in Hitler's cabinet (his team of 11 ministers). These conditions were meant to restrict Hitler's power, but it soon became clear that this would be harder than Hindenburg or Papen supposed. As he left the Palace Hitler cried out to some of his supporters, 'We've done it! We've done it!' On the following day he gave a speech which showed how confident he was:

Source 19.1 Over 14 years have passed since that unhappy day when the German people, blinded by promises made by those at home and abroad, forgot the highest values of our past, of the Reich [nation], of its honour and freedom and thereby lost everything...

The task before us is the most difficult which has faced German statesmen in living memory... The National Government will therefore regard it as its first and supreme task to restore to the German people unity of mind and will... Germany must not sink into Communist anarchy [lawlessness]...

The Marxist [Communist] parties and their followers had 14 years to prove their abilities. The result is a heap of ruins. Now, German people, give us four years and then judge us.

Source 19.2

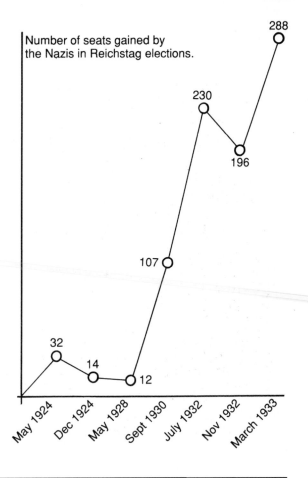

Number of seats gained by the Nazis in Reichstag elections.

Using the Evidence

1   When someone said he was worried about having Hitler as Chancellor Papen replied, 'Don't worry – we've hired him.' What do you think he meant by this?

2   Look at source 19.1. What 'unhappy day' is Hitler referring to? What values does he think were betrayed?

3   Look again at the last few lines of source 18.1 and compare it with source 19.1. Which of Hindenburg's fears appears to be justified? Why?

4   Suggest how different Germans might have felt when they heard Hitler's speech.

Coursework

Someone described a chart like the one above as 'the fever chart of the Weimar Republic'. What do you think he meant by this? What factors do you think caused the various changes you can see on the chart?

The Nazis were well-prepared to celebrate Hitler's success. They were experts at conducting rallies and had made arrangements for a victory rally in case their leader became the new Chancellor. Within a few hours of his success they held a magnificent torchlit rally in the centre of Berlin.

The following passages come from a diary. The writer, a woman called Frau Solmitz, lived in the German city of Hamburg. She mentions the Berlin rally then she writes about things that were happening in Hamburg. It soon becomes clear that she sees no danger in the Nazis' success:

Source 20.1

30 Jan. 1933
Hitler is Chancellor of the Reich! And what a cabinet!!! ... It is so incredibly marvellous that I an writing it down quickly before the first discordant note comes, for when has Germany ever experienced a blessed summer after a wonderful spring?

Huge torchlight processions in the presence of Hindenburg and Hitler by National Socialists and Stahlhelm [ex-servicemen's unofficial army] ... This is a memorable 30 January!

(Slightly re-arranged)

5 Feb. 1933
...the Reds waded through relentless rain – Gisela saw them with wives and children to make the procession longer. The Socialists and Reds will inevitably have to give in now

6 Feb. 1933
Torchlight procession of National Socialists and Stahlhelm! A wonderful... experience for all of us. Göring [a leading Nazi] says the day of Hitler's... appointment was something like 1914, and this too was something like 1914...

At 9.30 pm we took up our position, Gisela with us. I said she should stay to the end for the sake of the children... They should now have a really strong impression of nationhood, as we once had, and store it in their memories...

It was 10.00 pm by the time the first torches came, and then 20 000 brown shirts followed one another like waves in the sea; their faces shone with enthusiasm in the light of the torches. 'Three cheers for the Führer [leader], our Chancellor Adolf Hitler...' 'The Republic is shit.' 'The murderous reds have bloody hands and we won't forget...'

The SS brought up the rear of the procession. We were drunk with enthusiasm, blinded by the light of the torches right in our faces... And in front of us men, men, men, brightly coloured, grey, brown, a torrent lasting an hour and 20 minutes. In the wavering light of the torches one seemed to see only a few types recurring again and again, but there were between twenty-two and twenty-five thousand different faces!

Next to us a little boy of three kept raising his tiny hand: 'Heil Hitler, Heil Hitlerman!'

An SA man said to Gisela this morning: 'One doesn't say Heil Hitler any more, one says Heil Germany.' 'Death to the Jews' was also sometimes called out and they sang of the blood of the Jews which would squirt from their knives...

And these floods of people in Hamburg are only a small fraction of Hitler's support in the whole Reich.

Source 20.2 The SA and SS march in triumph through the Brandenburg gate, Berlin, in January 1933

___

Using the Evidence

1   Look at source 20.1. What sort of person does Solmitz seem to be?

2   Who do you think Solmitz means by 'the Reds'?

3   What sort of 'procession' do you think occurred on 5 February? (Think carefully about this and discuss it if necessary.) What attitude do you think Solmitz had to this procession?

4   In what form had some of the *Freikorps* survived?

5   What important event in German history occurred in 1914? (You may need to check this.) Why did Hitler's appointment and the victory celebrations remind his supporters of 1914?

6   Look at the first part of source 20.1 and suggest what warning Solmitz might have given the Nazis.

7   Who do you think Gisela is?
Try to explain why Solmitz wants her children to see the rally.

8   Who wore brown shirts? What title did they have for Hitler? When they say 'The Republic is shit' what are they referring to?

9   What effect do you think the Nazis wanted their rally to have? In the second half of source 20.1 what words does Solmitz use to describe its effect on the people around her?

___

21 The Reichstag Fire

On 27 February 1933 the Debating Chamber of the Reichstag was purposely set on fire. The blaze, which wrecked the Chamber completely, broke out after the Reichstag had been locked up for the night. Witnesses said they had seen someone breaking in through a window, and a Dutchman called Van der Lubbe was arrested in one of the corridors. He claimed that he had started the fire as a protest against injustice and poverty. However, Hitler had only just become Chancellor, and elections were due in seven days' time. An event like the fire could be used to influence voters' decisions, and the Nazis and Communists both tried to take advantage of it. Van der Lubbe was a Communist and the two sides accused each other of paying him to get involved. The Communists said that the fire was simply a Nazi plot to disgrace them in the voters' eyes. The Nazis said that the Communists deserved to be disgraced, since the fire was part of a Communist plot to take Germany over.

People still argue about what happened, and those who believe in a Nazi plot often claim that Göring was one of the ringleaders. Göring was the Reichstag's chairman (or 'Speaker'). His mansion was close to the Reichstag and the buildings were linked by an underground passage which carried the central heating pipes. According to one historian, a small detachment of storm-troopers used it to reach the Reichstag:

Source 21.1 They scattered petrol and self-igniting chemicals and then they made their way back to the [mansion]... At the same time a half-witted Dutch Communist with a passion for arson, Marinus van der Lubbe, had made his way into the huge, darkened and to him unfamiliar building and started a number of fires of his own... This was a godsend to the Nazis... [He] was arrested on the spot.

(W. Shirer, *The Rise and Fall of the Third Reich*, London, 1960)

Many cabinet members were told of the fire as soon as it started, and some of them dashed to the Reichstag to see what was going on. Because of the building's enormous size it was safe to go in, and Hitler was already talking about a Communist plot as he strode up the steps:

Source 21.2 'God grant,' he said, 'that this is the work of the Communists. You are now witnessing the beginning of a great new epoch in German history.' ... And a little later, when Papen appeared, Hitler seized his hand, shook it enthusiastically, and said, 'This is a God-given signal, Herr Vice-Chancellor! If this fire, as I believe, is the work of the Communists, then we must crush out this murderous pest with an iron fist.'

In the following passage Rudolph Diels, a policeman, describes how Hitler and some of 'his faithful' had gathered on a balcony overlooking the burning Chamber:

Source 21.3 Hitler was leaning over the stone parapet, gazing at a red ocean of fire. When I entered, Göring stepped towards me. His voice conveyed the full emotion of the fateful hour: 'This is the beginning of a Communist rising. Not a moment must be lost...'

Göring could not go on, for Hitler had swung round towards us all. I saw that his face had turned quite scarlet, both with excitement and also with the heat... Suddenly he started screaming at the top of his voice:

'Now we'll show them! Anyone who stands in our way will be mown down. The German people have been soft for too long. All Communist officials must be shot. All Communist deputies must be hanged this very night. All friends of the Communists must be locked up. And that goes for the Social Democrats... too.'

I reported on the results to the first interrogations of Marinus van der Lubbe – that in my opinion he was a maniac. But with this opinion I had come to the wrong man; Hitler ridiculed my childish view: 'This is something really cunning, prepared a long time ago. The criminals have thought all this out beautifully; but they've miscalculated, haven't they, Comrades!'

Hitler put his plan into action and many Communists fled from Germany. Others were rounded up and imprisoned or put to death. Van der Lubbe and three other Communists were charged with planning and starting the fire. Van der Lubbe pleaded guilty and he was sentenced to death; the other men were all set free. The Nazis had failed to prove that the fire was a Communist plot and arguments raged about whether the Dutchman had acted alone.

Source 21.5
Van der Lubbe at his trial

Source 21.4
The Reichstag debating chamber in ruins

There are three main ideas about who was behind the Reichstag fire. Each idea is summed up below with a brief quotation:

Was it the Nazis?

Göring described how 'the boys' had entered the Reichstag building by a subterranean passage... [On another occasion he said at a party] 'The only one who really knows about the Reichstag is I, for I set fire to it.' And saying this, he slapped his thigh.

(Quoted in F. Tobias, *The Reichstag Fire*, London, 1963)

Was it the Communists?

The court has established that van der Lubbe must have had accomplices [to start so many fires in the building]. The accomplices should be sought in the ranks of the Communist Party, and Communism is therefore guilty of the Reichstag fire.

(From van der Lubbe's trial, after others had been acquitted)

Was van der Lubbe acting alone?

As to the question whether I acted alone, I declare emphatically that this was the case. No one at all helped me, nor did I meet a single person in the Reichstag.

(From van der Lubbe's trial)

1   Look at source 21.1. Why would Nazi conspirators have been so pleased to arrest van der Lubbe?

2   The writer of source 21.1 goes on to say that van der Lubbe was 'a dupe of the Nazis'. How could this be?

3   Study source 21.2. What signs can you see that Hitler had not expected the fire? What does this suggest about its cause?

4   Why does Hitler say, 'God grant that it is the work of the Communists'?

5   Why do you think Hitler was so much more 'worked up' in source 21.3?

6   Van der Lubbe claimed to have set fire to the Reichstag curtains with his blazing jacket, but the court tested samples of the material which had been stored in a chest. They refused to burn, and the court concluded that accomplices must have 'primed' the curtains with chemicals. What weakness can you see in this?

7   What different accounts does Göring give about who was responsible for the fire? Which do you trust least? Why?

8   The writer of source 21.1 must have relied on 'primary sources' (things that were written by witnesses). He was not a witness himself so his work is a 'secondary source'. What sort of source is best if you want to make up your mind about the facts? Why do you think so?

9   Do *you* think van der Lubbe acted independently? Discuss this with friends, and try to give reasons for the verdict you reach.

4 Nazi Dictatorship

22 An End to Freedom and Democracy

On the night of the Reichstag fire, Hitler had ordered many arrests and executions. However, he had no right to do this, since the law protected people's liberty. Only those convicted of crimes in German courts could be shot, hanged or thrown into jail. On the following day, Hitler and his cabinet changed the law so that Hitler's orders could be carried out. The new law, called the Decree for the Preservation of People and State, restricted:

– free speech
– freedom of the press
– people's right to have public meetings
– the power of the state authorities.

The new law also permitted:

– imprisonment without trial
– vetting of mail and telephone calls
– searches of homes and business premises
– confiscation of property.

The Reichstag was making arrangements to meet in an opera house while the fire-damaged building was being repaired. However, the cabinet approved the Decree without consulting the Reichstag members. Under the German constitution the cabinet were free to do this in a national emergency, but was there a real emergency?
 In truth there had probably been no Communist plot to take the country over. Hitler used the idea of a plot to justify making his Decree; news of the Decree then added to the shock and confusion which the fire had caused, convincing people that a Communist plot had been discovered just in time.
 The Decree was quickly put into effect:

Source 22.1 This was... Nazi terror backed up by the government. Truckloads of storm-troopers roared through the streets all over Germany, breaking into homes, rounding up victims and carting them off to SA barracks, where they were tortured and beaten. The Communist press and political meetings were suppressed; ... the meetings of the democratic parties either banned or broken up. Only the Nazis and their Nationalist allies were permitted to campaign unmolested.

(W. Shirer, *The Rise and Fall of the Third Reich*, London, 1960)

Campaigning was going on because elections were due on 5 May. The elections took place in an atmosphere of crisis and anxiety, and the Nazis gained more seats than ever. The number rose from 196 to 288. Papen's Nationalist Party gained only 52 seats, but between them they and the Nazis had a slender majority in the Reichstag. Although his position was stronger than ever Hitler was still not satisfied. He wanted to do away with the Reichstag so that he and his cabinet could make decisions without its approval. This would involve a change in the German Constitution, and such a change had to be passed by a two to one majority in the Reichstag. But why should the deputies stand for election then promptly vote themselves out of office? The Nazis were willing to do so since they favoured dictatorial rule by Hitler, their leader. The Nazis' Nationalist allies were also prepared to support the move, and the Catholic Centre Party agreed to support it after Hitler had given them various bribes and empty promises. There were two other main groups of deputies, the Communists and the Social Democrats. Both of these were hostile to Hitler, and between them they might have blocked his attempt to suspend the Reichstag. However, the Communist deputies had been arrested or forced into hiding. As a result, they could not take up their seats in the Reichstag, and the Social Democrats had to try and speak for them all. This required enormous courage:

Source 22.2 Hitler read out his government declaration in a surprisingly calm voice. Only in a few places did he raise it to a fanatical frenzy: at the end of his speech he uttered dark threats of what would happen if the

Reichstag did not support the Enabling Act he was demanding...

Otto Wels read out our reply. With his voice half choking, he gave our good wishes to the persecuted and oppressed in the country who, though innocent, were already filling the prisons and prison camps simply on account of their political creed.

This speech made a terrifying impression on all of us. Only a few hours before we had heard that members of the SA had taken away a 45-year-old welfare worker..., stripped her completely, bound her on a table and flogged her body with leather whips. The female members of our group were in tears; some sobbed uncontrollably...

We tried to dam the flood of Hitler's unjust accusations with cries of 'No!', 'An error!', 'False!' But that did us no good. The SA and SS people, who surrounded us in a semicircle along the walls of the hall, hissed loudly and murmered: 'Shut up!', 'Traitors!', 'You'll be strung up today'.

(Quoted in Noakes and Pridham, *Documents on Nazism 1919–45*, London, 1974, and found in N. Richardson, *The Third Reich*, London, 1987)

At the end of the session the 84 Social Democrats voted against the Bill but 441 other deputies voted for it. Hitler had needed a two to one majority but he won by over five to one.

German soldiers round up spies during Hitler's purge

1   What did Hitler call the rules by which he restricted freedom? Why do you think he chose such a title?

2   How do you think Germans heard about the new rules? Do you think their sources of information were fair or biased? Why?

3   Suggest how different Germans might have felt when they heard about the rules or saw them being carried out.

4   Look at source 22.1 and other extracts from Shirer's work, such as source 21.1. What attitude do you think Shirer has to the Nazis? How might this affect your use of his work?

5   Who was Otto Wels? What 'innocent' people was he referring to in source 22.2? Which of these people did he and his colleagues know?

6   Why did Wels and his colleagues feel frightened during the meeting?

7   What did Hitler achieve with his Enabling Bill?

23   Censorship and Propaganda

The elections of 1933 were the last to be held for many years. Hitler took away more and more of the Germans' rights, tightening his dictatorship and creating a *totalitarian state* – a state where the ruler or the ruling group controls people's lives as completely as possible. Through his censors, Hitler controlled what people read and what they heard on the radio. Newspapers which opposed the Nazis were quickly closed down, and only official radio stations were allowed on the air. Hitler also controlled what people heard and saw in theatres and cinemas, and he even tried to control what the clergy told them in church.

   Many books and authors were banned, and the SA organised giant bonfires where thousands of books went up in flames. Everything written by Jewish authors came under the ban, and the great Jewish scientist, Albert Einstein, was forced to leave Germany.

Source 23.1
Nazi daubings
on a Jewish
shop window

The ban on books by Jews fitted in with the Nazis' anti-semitic policies, under which Jews were barred from jobs like teaching, and sometimes even from food-shops and doctors' surgeries. However, Nazi censorship was mainly designed to stop people questioning Nazi policies. No one, whatever his race, could express political views which conflicted with those which the Nazis laid down. All this meant that the Germans did not have the chance to share alternative viewpoints and think for themselves.

A man called Joseph Goebbels was in charge of censorship and propaganda. Propaganda consists of choosing and twisting news and ideas in order to influence public attitudes. The Nazis had done it successfully when they published news of the Reichstag fire.

By that time they were already beginning to dominate the press and radio. Besides excluding things they disliked, they were turning the press and radio into channels of Nazi propaganda.

In the summer of 1933 the Nazis made a further move to dominate people's lives and thoughts. Through his cabinet, Hitler declared that only one political party would now be allowed:

Source 23.3 The Nationalist Socialist German Workers' Party constitutes the only political party in Germany... Whoever undertakes to maintain the organisation of another political party or to form a new political party will be punished with penal servitude...

Source 23.2
A night-time gathering of Nazi officials and supporters to burn books

1 What is happening in source 23.2?

2 How can you tell that the bonfire has been organised by the Nazis?

3 Do you think the Nazis would have been happy for source 23.2 to be published in Germany? Do you think they would have been happy for it to appear in other countries? In each case say why you think so.

4 Someone has said, 'If you start burning books you end up burning people.' Why should this be true?

---

24 The Night of the Long Knives

Although it supported Nazi policies Hitler felt uneasy about the SA and its growing strength. Under its Chief of Staff, Ernst Röhm, it was gaining many new recruits. Its numbers had risen from half a million in 1930 to two and a half million by the end of 1933. Röhm pointed out that the SA was a genuine 'People's Army'; it was larger than the official army and could easily replace or absorb it. Röhm was eager for this to happen, and he also wanted to gain control of the *Stahlhelm* and the SS (Hitler's bodyguard). The Minister of Defence, General von Blomberg, was very suspicious of Röhm's ambitions and felt that his own position was threatened. Army officers also felt under serious threat; they did not want to lose their status or see their units absorbed into larger SA battalions.

The officers were an influential group of men whose support was probably crucial to the Nazis' success. The Nazis also needed support (and money) from Germany's landowning class, most of whom favoured the army and not the SA thugs. Factors like these encouraged Hitler to side with the army. In addition, he was afraid that Röhm and the SA would try to overthrow him, along with the rest of the party leadership. There was intense rivalry between the SA and local party leaders; the SA sometimes mocked them for wearing uniforms which had never been on a battlefield. With their bright metal fittings the uniforms looked so crisp and new that the SA accused the wearers of having fallen off a Christmas tree.

By April 1934, Hitler felt that the time had come to deal with the SA once and for all. He also had a positive reason to favour the army. Hindenburg, who was 96, was very ill and was likely to die within a few months. Under the German constitution, the President had important powers, and when he died these powers would pass to the person elected as his successor. Hitler wanted unrestricted power for himself, and he therefore decided to take over Hindenburg's powers when he died. He would then combine the roles – and the powers – of Chancellor and President. Hitler realised that he would need the forces' support if he was to do such a thing, and he therefore made a bargain with the leaders of the army and navy. He promised to deal with Röhm and other SA leaders; he would also reduce the SA's size, enlarge the army and guarantee its status as Germany's main fighting force. In return, the army and navy leaders would support Hitler's move to seize Hindenburg's powers.

This was a difficult time for Hitler, since many groups in Germany, including land and factory owners, were protesting about the harshness of the Nazis' regime. There were calls for an end to persecution, censorship, strongarm tactics and mass arrests. Papen had helped to bring Hitler to power. However, in June he gave a speech in which he protested about the lack of freedom in Hitler's Germany:

Source 24.1 Open manly discussions would be of more service to the German people than, for instance, the present state of the German press. The government must be mindful of the old maxim, 'Only weaklings suffer no criticism' ... Great men are not created by propaganda... It is only by talking things over with people that confidence and devotion can be maintained. People treated as morons have no confidence to give... It is time... to silence fanatics.

(Found in W. Shirer, *The Rise and Fall of the Third Reich*, London, 1960)

The speech was reported in certain papers, though Goebbels did his best to suppress it. Hitler responded by calling Papen 'a pygmy who imagines he can stop, with a few phrases, the gigantic renewal of a people's life.'

Just before dawn on Saturday 30 June, SS men went into action. They pounced on leading members of the SA, most of whom were asleep in their beds, and shot them or stabbed them. The killings went on for 36 hours, and the Saturday night is usually known as 'The Night of the Long Knives'. According to Hitler, 77 men were killed, including three who 'committed suicide'. Later estimates put the number at more than 1000. Röhm was certainly one of the victims, and the SS also murdered several politicians. Papen was placed under house arrest but his office was ransacked and several

of his staff were killed. Hitler had kept his bargain with the forces' chiefs and had also dealt with some of his critics.

He later explained to the Reichstag that the SA had been on the point of launching an armed revolt:

Source 24.3 The call to action had already come. Action was to begin with a surprise attack, the government buildings were to be occupied... This was mutiny!... In these circumstances I could make but one decision... Only a ruthless and bloody intervention might still perhaps stifle the spread of revolt...

(Found in W. Shirer, *The Rise and Fall of the Third Reich*, London, 1960)

Hitler had earned the army's support in his bid to take over Hindenburg's powers. Hindenburg died on 2 August and the army kept its part of the bargain. It raised no objection when the cabinet declared that Hitler was now the

Source 24.2 A cartoon from a British paper

THEY SALUTE WITH BOTH HANDS NOW.

President as well as the Chancellor, and the officers and men took the following oath of loyalty to him:

Source 24.4 I swear by God this sacred oath: I will render unconditional obedience to Adolf Hitler, the Führer of the German nation and people, Supreme Commander of the Armed Forces, and will be ready as a brave soldier to risk my life at any time for this oath.

Public officials had to swear a similar oath. Hitler now had absolute power, and the title Führer, which he used more and more, sums up his authority.

It was now very hard indeed to organise any sort of opposition to Hitler. The Nazis' domination of the media (and their secret police) meant that anti-Nazi feeling was restricted to separate groups, and sometimes they did not even know of each other's existence.

For the most part, people were satisfied with Hitler and the Nazis. News reports (which Goebbels controlled) spoke of great success in foreign policy, and German people were certainly becoming prosperous. To their delight, Hitler had kept his promise and stopped paying reparations to Belgium and France. It seemed that Germany was once again a great and proud nation, and people with well-paid jobs in weapons factories had no complaints about Germany's rapid rearmament.

Using the Evidence

1   When Papen said 'It is time to silence fanatics' who do you think he meant? How well does the idea of silencing people fit in with the rest of what he said?

2   Why do you think Hitler chose the word 'pygmy' when responding to Papen?

3   Look at source 24.2. What do you think the artist was saying?

4   Whose 'action' and 'intervention' is Hitler referring to in source 24.3? Why do you think he calls it 'ruthless and bloody' rather than keeping quiet about this?

5   Hitler invited the German people to vote on his action in combining the roles of Chancellor and President. They did so on 19 August 1934 and approved it overwhelmingly. How far do you think this justifies what Hitler had done? What reservations do you have?

---

25   The Berlin Olympics

In 1936 the Olympic Games were held in Berlin. Athletes, reporters and other foreign visitors crowded into the city, and many were struck by the Germans' careful preparations:

Source 25.1 I crossed the frontier into Germany to be greeted by... a banner inscribed 'Welcome!' and decked with the five symbolic rings of the Olympic Games.

With those rings I was soon to be bored... In Berlin they were everywhere – on trams, buses, menus, shop windows; they were stamped on my passport...; they appeared, of course, on the White Olympic standard which fluttered beside the Swastika flag over so many houses; they sprouted, in metal, from buttonholes, hats and blouses. Every possible space had its Olympic rings – with one surprising exception. The [sides] of the zoo elephants had somehow been overlooked...

The Nazis [were determined] that a good time should be had by all. If Swastika banners monopolised [some of the avenues], elsewhere his national flag flapped at every turn before the visiting foreigner. An

Englishman could contemplate the Union Jack...

The Berliners – encouraged, I believe, by injunctions [commands] from high places – bubbled over with courtesy. They made you feel that your presence was a great honour, and that your comfort was their most pressing ambition...

In the midst of all this hospitality, however, certain doubts were always with me. I could not forget that many people in England consider Germany's... nationalism the chief obstacle to European peace, and I reminded myself that in a corporate State a few smiles and handshakes from individuals mean nothing at all. Presently the smiles might become frowns, and the hand now open might be clenched at the will of the ruling clique [group], for it is they, not the common people, who are the ultimate arbiters [deciders] of policy. There can be no doubt that if, or when, Herr Hitler says 'Fight!' – for whatever cause – the Germans will reply with [a] disciplined 'Ja!'

(Philip Stockil, The *Yorkshire Post*, 8 August 1936)

One American writer dared to suggest that cruel signs attacking Jews had suddenly disappeared from the streets. He later wrote that the German authorities nearly threw him out of the country for saying this. Most foreign visitors gained a very good impression of life in Germany:

Source 25.2 Visitors... came away enormo impressed... by the fact that life seemed t on as pleasantly as in any other Europ country. Many of them concluded that tales they had heard about persecution Jews, Catholics and political dissidents n have been grossly exaggerated, for as t moved around Berlin or drove freely thro the country they saw no signs of harassm besides, the ordinary people they met w hospitable and kind. They came ho convinced that the Nazi regime was far black than it had been painted...

It was a triumph of bluff and propagano by the Führer himself, executed largely by genius of his Minister for Propaganda, Jos Goebbels...

During the Games there was no sir report of a foreign visitor being insulted racial grounds. Neither Jewish athletes blacks were harassed or made to feel in least degree unwelcome: on the contrary, newcomers were received w overwhelming hospitality.

(D. Hart-Davis, *Hitler's Olympics*, London 1

Some news reports which appeared at the tim gave a slightly different idea of how foreign athletes were treated:

Source 25.3 After an impressive ceremony which Herr Hitler, General Göring and otl Nazi leaders were present, the Olym Games were brought to a conclusion... T crowd cheered Herr Hitler and there w repeated shouts of 'Heil!' Then followed singing of the National Anthem and the Naz song.

The organisation of the Games has be magnificent. The one criticism to be ma concerns the over-ardent support the Germ public gave its own competitors. They ratl allowed nationalism to run away with the Germany, in the third place of an event, h far more applause than winners of otl nationalities, no matter how excellent t winner's performance was.

(The *Yorkshire Post*, 17 August 19

Hitler and other Germans seemed especially reluctant to applaud Jesse Owens. Owens, an American, was one of the Games' most successful competitors, winning three gold medals and helping his country to win a fourth in the relay race.

Hitler at the
Olympic Games

In a splendid struggle Erwin Siestas, a German was beaten by a Japanese, T. Hamuro in the 200 m breaststoke

Jesse Owens

1   What was Goebbels' job in Nazi Germany? How did he and Hitler exploit the Berlin Olympics?

2   What do you think Philip Stockil meant by 'a corporate State'? (Use the next few lines of the passage to help you answer this.) What danger did he see in Germany being 'a corporate State'?

3   Look at source 25.2 and source 25.3. What features do you think would have worried Philip Stockil?

4   In deciding whether black athletes were treated warmly would you give more weight to source 25.2 or to news reports like source 25.3? Why?

5   Why might the Germans have been upset by Owens' successes?

26   Churches and Schools

The Nazis had banned many organisations which might have opposed them. However, the churches had too much support from the German people to be closed down. Their international links also gave them considerable power and influence. The Nazis therefore decided to turn the churches into allies rather than quarrelling with them. They had to deal with the Roman Catholics (who made up a third of German Christians) and also with the Protestants (who made up the rest).

The Protestant churches had been founded in the sixteenth century under the influence of a monk and scholar called Martin Luther. Like many other men of his time, Luther was viciously anti-Jewish. He said that Jews should be thrown out onto the streets to beg. He also said that respectable citizens should support the civil (or state) authorities. Like other Germans, many clergy accepted Luther's anti-semitic attitudes and also his love of stern authority. Needless to say, this suited the Nazis very well.

Hitler wanted to bind the Protestant churches into a single 'Reich Church' under Nazi control. The churches would then be unable to organise opposition to Nazi rule. They would even have to change what they taught to fit in with National Socialism. The Bible was the Christians' holy book, yet a leading Nazi called Reinhardt Krause suggested that they should abandon most of it. He also said that the parts that contained the teachings of Christ should be rewritten to 'match the demands of National Socialism'. Krause led a Nazi-style rally for

Christians who shared his ideas. Those who attended it took an oath of allegiance to Hitler. They also demanded that people should not be allowed in church if they did not belong to the 'German race'.

This was too much for a clergyman called Martin Niemöller. He and other clergy formed an anti-Nazi branch of the church called the Confessional Church. They also formed 'the Pastors' Emergency League' for clergy opposed to the Nazis. Acts like these required great courage, for the SA often called at their homes in the dead of night. Some men were simply beaten up, while others were taken away and imprisoned. Despite their suffering, Niemöller and his colleagues felt that they were succeeding. The existence of the Confessional Church meant that Hitler had failed to unite the Protestant churches and bring them all under Nazi control.

At the end of 1935 the Confessional Church was declared illegal. This did not automatically put an end to its activities. However, it meant that arrests could be carried out openly, and in greater numbers than ever before. In the late 1930s hundreds of clergy and lay members of the Confessional Church were thrown into prison. Niemöller was among the victims, and he spent over seven years in custody.

Some clergy who had opposed the Nazis were frightened by the level of beatings and imprisonments. In the end they nearly all gave in to Nazi demands and took an oath of allegiance to Hitler. This meant that they could be forced to spread whatever religious teachings he wanted.

The Nazis drew up documents setting out their

plans for German religion:

Source 26.1 The national church will clear away from its altars all crosses and Bibles; ...

On the altars there must be nothing but *Mein Kampf* (to the German nation and therefore to God the most sacred book) and to the left of the altar a sword; ...

The Christian cross must be... replaced by the only unconquerable symbol, the swastika.

(From the 30-point programme for the 'National Reich Church' by Rosenberg, 1941 quoted in W. Shirer, The Rise and Fall of the Third Reich, London, 1960)

In some Nazi writings there were hints that Hitler was a god or a prophet. For example, Hitler's Minister of Church Affairs described him as 'the herald of a new revelation'.

The Nazis never carried out their plans to 'Nazify' worship in Protestant churches. They were too concerned with getting the churches' support for their policies (or at least stamping out opposition). It was even harder to bring the Roman Catholic Church under full state control,

Source 26.2 Churches often gave their blessing to the Hitler Youth

since it belonged to a worldwide organisation based in Rome. Like Protestants, Roman Catholics had various views of the Nazi régime. Many preferred the Nazis to the Communists, who rejected organised religion completely. Others felt that Nazi policies violated Christian principles. Several Roman Catholic bishops spoke out against what the Nazis were doing:

Source 26.3 Several times a week buses arrive in Hadamar with a considerable number of victims. Schoolchildren of the neighbourhood know the vehicle and say, 'There comes the murder-box again.' After the arrival of the vehicle, the citizens of Hadamar watch the smoke rising from the chimney and are tormented by the constant thought of the miserable victims, especially when they are sickened by repulsive smells, depending on the direction of the wind.

The effects of the whole operation here are these: Children call one another names and say, 'You're loony, you'll be sent to the baking oven in Hadamar.' ... You hear old folks say, 'Don't send me to a State hospital. After the

feeble-minded have been finished off, it'll be the turn of the next lot who eat more than they're worth – the old people.' ...

The official notice that So-and-so had died of a contagious disease and that for that reason his body has had to be burned is now met with plain disbelief...

(A letter from Bishop Hilfrith of Limburg to the German Minister of Justice, 13 August 1941)

Source 26.4 A Jewish child being shamed in a classroom

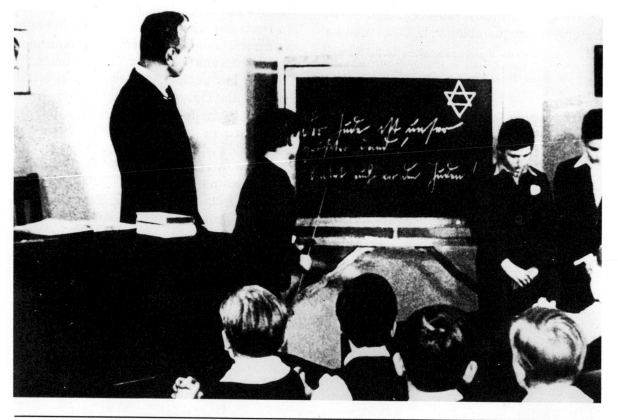

_____ **Using the Evidence** _____

1   Using the information in this section, list three or four feelings which Christians (and others) had about the Nazis.

2   Why do you think the Nazis wanted to change the way in which people worshipped?

3   Look at source 26.3. What happens to the people who are brought to Hadamar? Who are the victims?

4   What do people in Hadamar fear will happen next?

5   Why do you think the Bishop refers to people's reactions, rather than just complaining about what is going on?

6   Why do you think the Nazis had such a policy?

Hitler Youth on parade

5 Expansion of Germany

THE YORKSHIRE POST

FRANCE WILL NOT CO

INDEX AND SUMMARY

FOREIGN

German troops on Saturday entered the Rhineland Demilitarised Zone in defiance of the Treaty of Locarno and of the Versailles Peace Treaty. Pages 9 and 10

A French Note requesting a meeting of the League Council reached Geneva yesterday. It states that Germany has violated her engagements, and asks for a meeting of the Council as soon as possible. Page 9

Broadcasting to the French people last night M. Sarraut, the Prime Minister, declared that France will refuse to examine the new proposals put forward by Herr Hitler. Page 9

Germany's action has aroused world-wide comment. A section of the French Press urges that the League must apply sanctions against the Reich. Page 9

THE WAR

PREMIER'S REPLY TO VIOLATION

LEAGUE COUNCIL MEETING ON FRIDAY

BRITISH GOVERNMENT STATEMENT TO-DAY

10,000 GERMAN TROOPS NOW IN DEMILITARISED ZONE

France refuses to examine the new proposals put forward by Herr Hitler, and has asked for an early meeting of the League Council to consider the situation arising out of Germany's re-occupation of the demilitarised Rhineland Zone.

THIS declaration was made by M. Sarraut, the French Prime Minister, in a broadcast to the nation last night dealing with Germany's repudiation of Locarno and her new violation of the Treaty of Versailles.

He declared that Germany had violated treaties in the past, and that France refused to negotiate under the menace of troops in the Rhineland.

The text of France's Note to the League is given on this page. The League Council has been summoned to meet on Friday. Germany also has been invited to attend, but it is expected that she will let the invitation go by default.

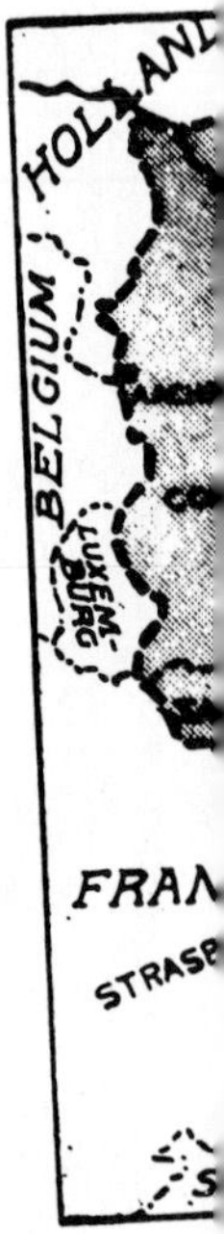

St

B

SERIC
OF

Dec

MR.

immedi
situatio
Germa
Rhinel

9

AY, MARCH 9, 1936

DER HITLER'S OFFERS

IND'
CASSEL
ANKFURT
IZ
NHEIM
SRUHE
RG
ID

NE WORLD VIEWS ON NAZI MOVE

French Press Call for Sanctions

SOVIET FEARS

"Peace Endangered in Western Europe"

VIEWS in foreign capitals on Germany's isolation of Locarno are summed up in the following Reuter telegrams:—

France

PARIS, Sunday

The entire Paris Press is at one this morning in expressing indignation at the German repudiation of Locarno and the latest violation of the Treaty of Versailles. The argument that the responsibility for the German action lies upon the Franco-Soviet Pact is energetically rejected.

M. Saint-Brice remarks in the "Journal":—

"Once more Germany defies the world. But the haste of Hitler, who flatters himself that he is manœuvring between London, Paris and Rome, may afford an opportunity for the indispensable gathering together again of the bloc for the maintenance of order.

"It is no longer a question of preventing the evil, as when Signor Mussolini mobilised his troops in the Brenner. We have to deal with a *fait accompli*. Shall we dare to take sanctions against Germany?"

Suggested Boycott

After declaring that a policy of illusion and weakness has been followed for ten years past regarding Germany, and that it is now bearing fruit, "Pertinax" in the "Echo de Paris" discusses the sanctions which he says the League must apply. He says:—

"The economy of Hitler's Germany is extremely fragile. The Reichsbank possesses very little gold. A ban on the purchase of German goods would be a fairly severe blow. A network of military agreements must express the solidarity of the Sanctionist Powers."

FRANCE MANS BORDER FORTRESSES

"We Will Not Leave Strasbourg Under German Gunfire"

PREMIER'S DECLARATION TO THE NATION

PARIS, Sunday

THE decision that the German Memorandum was unacceptable was taken at a Ministerial Council this morning, and a statement is to be made to Parliament at the opening of Tuesday's sitting.

The Council also approved the decision to bring Germany's action before the Council forthwith, and authorised the Ministers of War, Marine and Air to take such additional steps as the situation demanded.

France's Eastern Rhine frontier presented a busy scene to-day as troops and officers returned from their cancelled leave to their posts in the garrisons and forts of the formidable "Maginot line."

At Kehl, near Strasbourg, the French and German troops are now separated only by the span of a single bridge, instead of by a demilitarised 31 miles.

The population, however, is everywhere reported to be calm, and a Franco-German football match at Metz was played this afternoon according to plan—though with few spectators and a special guard of gendarmes.

No New Classes Called Up

Messages from the frontier towns and information from the War Ministry show that this tightening up of the Eastern defences has not involved the calling up of any fresh military classes, or even the introduction of fresh troops into the salient points.

It was stated at the War Ministry that the measures taken to-day and yesterday were purely local, and had already been foreseen some days ago.

At Strasbourg all the garrison are confined to their barracks or their fortified positions. No reinforcements have been introduced from outside Alsace. On the French side of the international bridge at Kehl, however, the guards have been reinforced, and innumerable telephone lines

more peace in Europe, no more international relations if this method becomes generalised.

Serving Interests of Europe

"In refusing to accept it we are serving the interests of the European community.

"The bare fact that, in defiance of solemn engagements, the German soldier has established himself on the banks of the Rhine also prohibits negotiation. After mature consideration I declare, on behalf of the French Government, that we mean to maintain essential guarantees of French and Belgian security, countersigned by the British and Italian Governments in the Treaty of Locarno.

We are not ready to leave Strasbourg under German gunfire. Our cause is just and strong. In defending it we are conscious of defending with our destiny an essential element of European peace. The French people realises this, and will, we know, unanimously support the Government's action.

"The German Government," added the Premier, "think they have well chosen their moment for the *coup de force*—the electoral period which has virtually opened in France. They are reckoning on a national upheaval born of our intestinal strife. That is the true explanation of the German Government's sudden decision.

"They have forgotten that at every grave hour in our history such upheavals have been dissipated in the immediate union of all parties in defence of national independence and security."

There was little diplomatic activity in Paris to-day. The British Ambassador, Sir George Clerk, saw M. Leger, Secretary-General of the Quai d'Orsay, but only regarding Mr. Eden's time-table on Tuesday, which is as a matter of fact not yet fixed up. M. Flandin saw Signor Cerruti and the United States Ambassador. It has been decided that M. Paul-Boncour, Minister for League Affairs, will represent France at the meeting of the Committee of Eighteen at Geneva on Tuesday. M. Flandin has to be present in the French Chamber in the afternoon of that day for the Government declaration on Hitler's move. He must also attend Thurs-

ent

Eden

H VIEW ACTION

o Nazi dor

eign Secretary. tement in the mmons to-day, stions, on the the entry of e Demilitarised

_____ **Using the Evidence** _____

1   Look at the newspaper report and the photograph. What happened? Why does the newspaper link it with the Treaty of Versailles?

2   What are governments doing about the situation? Why do you think they feel so strongly?

3   How do you think civilians feel? (The report in column five of the paper will probably give you some ideas.)

_____ **Coursework** _____

Design a newspaper front page showing how you think the German action might have been reported in Germany. Write out one report in full and use headlines to give an idea of what the others might say.

German troops after crossing the Rhine

Since the nineteenth century, Germans had often disagreed about how large Germany ought to be. Some of them wanted a 'larger Germany', which would have included neighbouring areas like Austria which were German-speaking and German in culture. Many other Germans were content with a 'smaller Germany' which had existed up to 1919. As we have seen, this 'smaller Germany' became smaller still when territories were taken away from it by the Treaty of Versailles. Most Germans wanted these territories back, and those who believed in a 'larger Germany' also wanted union with Austria.

In one of his speeches Hitler referred to the Austrians and to the Germans living in Czechoslovakia:

Source 28.1 Over ten million Germans live in two of the states adjoining our frontiers... It is unbearable for a world power to know there are racial comrades at its side who are constantly being afflicted with the severest suffering for their sympathy or unity with the whole nation... To the German Reich belongs the protection of those German peoples who are not in a position to secure... their political and spiritual freedom by their own efforts.

(Quoted in W.Shirer, *The Rise and Fall of the Third Reich*, London, 1960)

The Nazi party had been banned in Austria and some of its leading members had been imprisoned. In 1938 Hitler told the Austrian Chancellor, Kurt von Schuschnigg, to lift the ban and release the imprisoned party members. He also told him to include a man called Arthur Seyss-Inquart in his cabinet. Seiss-Inquart supported Nazi policies, and Hitler said he should be in charge of law and order.

Hitler gave Schuschnigg four days to consider these demands. While he did so German propaganda broadcasts carried 'false, but credible news' of German plans to march into Austria. A German general mentioned the broadcasts in his diary:

Source 28.2 The effect is quick and strong. In Austria the impression is created that Germany is undertaking serious military preparations.

(General Jodl, quoted in W. Shirer, *The Rise and Fall of the Third Reich*, London, 1960)

Under this pressure the Austrian government quickly accepted Hitler's demands. However, Schuschnigg gave a defiant speech in the Austrian Parliament in which he declared that Austria must now stand firm and safeguard its freedom. He ended with the slogan 'Red-white-red until we're dead.' He was referring to the colours of the Austrian flag, but during his speech crowds of Nazis had gathered in various towns. They tore down Austrian flags and replaced them with Swastika banners. Seiss-Inquart was now responsible for law and order, so nothing was done to quell the Nazis' riotous behaviour. Some town councils had put up loudspeakers so that people could listen to Chancellor Schuschnigg. Soon the loudspeakers were being crushed under Nazi boots – or were booming out Nazi propaganda.

In a last attempt to preserve his country's independence Schuschnigg decided to find out by referendum whether his people favoured 'a free, independent, social, Christian and united Austria'. However, on 11 March, two days before the referendum was due to take place, Schuschnigg was told that German troops were gathering just across the border. This time the military threat was real, and Schuschnigg felt that all he could do was cancel the referendum and resign as Chancellor.

The Nazis were still not satisfied, for the Austrian President, Wilhelm Miklas, refused to follow suit and resign. Hitler therefore ordered his troops to cross the border and show their strength. As they poured into Austria, Göring, the German General, instructed Seyss-Inquart to send the following telegram:

Source 28.3 The provisional Austrian government sends to the German Government the urgent request to support it in its task and to help it to prevent bloodshed. For this purpose it asks the German Government to send German troops as soon as possible.

(Quoted in W. Shirer, *The Rise and Fall of the Third Reich*, London, 1960)

Hitler was certainly keen that there should be no bloodshed:

Source 28.4 The behaviour of the troops must

give the impression that we do not want to wage war against our Austrian brothers. It is in our own interests that the whole operation shall be carried out without violence but in the form of a peaceful entry well received by the population. Therefore any provocation is to be avoided.

(Quoted in W. Shirer, *The Rise and Fall of the Third Reich*, London, 1960)

As Hitler had hoped, the invasion was a peaceful affair – an excellent show of Nazi strength and discipline. Seyss-Inquart became the Chancellor and President, combining the roles just as Hitler had done in Germany. On 13 March Seyss-Inquart approved a document which had been prepared by Hitler himself.

It included the words 'Austria is a province of the German Reich'. A new referendum was organised so that the Austrians and Germans could give their approval. They were simply asked whether or not they approved of the Anschluss (union).

Hitler spent the next four weeks campaigning in Austrian and German cities. He wanted an overwhelming vote in favour of the union, and in some of his speeches he claimed that he was carrying out the will of God:

Source 28.5 I believe that it was God's will to send a youth from here into the Reich to let him grow up, to raise him to be the leader of the nation so as to enable him to lead back his homeland into the Reich.

(Found in W. Shirer, *The Rise and Fall of the Third Reich*, London, 1960)

It is hard to be sure what the Austrian people really felt about Hitler's actions:

Source 28.6 In a fair and honest election in which the Social Democrats and Schuschnigg's Christian Socialists would have had freedom to campaign openly the plebiscite [referendum], in my opinion, might have been close. As it was, it took a very brave Austrian to vote No. As in Germany, and not without reason, the voters feared that their failure to

German troops in Austria

cast an affirmative vote might be found out. In the polling station which I visited in Vienna that Sunday afternoon, wide slits in the corner of the polling booths gave the Nazi election committee sitting a few feet away a good view of how one voted. In the country districts few bothered – or dared – to cast their ballots in the secrecy of the booth, they voted openly for all to see... A Nazi official assured me... that the Austrians were voting 99 per cent *Ja*. That was the figure officially given later...

(W. Shirer, *The Rise and Fall of the Third Reich*, London, 1960)

Using the Evidence

1 In the first half of source 28.1 which three countries does Hitler refer to? How does he describe Germany?

2 What reason or reasons does Hitler give for 'protecting' Germans who are outside Germany's frontiers? What does he mean by 'the whole nation'?

3 Germans were in a minority in Czechoslovakia but they made up nearly all the population in Austria. How might this lead you to question the second sentence in source 28.1?

4 What false reports were broadcast to the Austrians? Why was this done?

5 How might Schuschnigg's referendum have helped to preserve Austria's independence?

6 Why do you think Göring wanted Seyss-Inquart to send the telegram (source 28.3)?

7 How did Hitler want his troops to behave in Austria? Why do you think he wanted this?

8 Why do you think Hitler had the union of Austria approved by referendum? Why do you think he refused to use the wording which Schuschnigg had chosen?

9 In source 28.5 who do you think the 'youth' was? Why do you think Hitler spoke in this way?

10 At the start of source 28.6 how does Shirer hint that the Nazis hindered free speech in Austria?

11 Why do you think many country people felt safer voting openly than secretly?

12 Look at the last few lines of source 28.6. Suggest one or two reasons why the Nazi official's 'assurance' might be rather suspicious.

Coursework

Pretend that you are the Nazi official and write your own account of the voting.

As soon as the Austrian crisis was over attention turned to the part of Czechoslovakia called the Sudetenland. The Sudeten people were German-speaking and German in culture. They wanted the region to pass from Czech to German control. Their Nazi Party, which took its instructions direct from Hitler and his Foreign Minister, Joachim von Ribbentrop, organised campaigns and illegal activities to prepare the way for a German takeover.

Hitler being welcomed by the Sudeten Germans

The British and French were alarmed at rumours of German plans to take the Sudetenland by force. The French had friendly relations with Czechoslovakia and were bound by treaties to help the Czechs if their country ever came under attack. They feared that they would soon be drawn into a war against Germany. As allies of the French, the British feared that they, too, might become involved. They were also afraid that the Germans might conquer the whole of Czechoslovakia and then go on to conquer the rest of south-east Europe, thus threatening British trade and power in the Mediterranean.

According to British and German spokesmen, 'It would be the height of folly if [Britain and Germany] were to exterminate each other in war, since this would open the way to Communism...'. However, by September 1938 there seemed little doubt that war would occur. During that month the British Prime Minister, Neville Chamberlain, flew to Germany three times to try to settle the crisis. Hitler assured him that the Sudetenland was the final piece of territory he would claim but he also insisted that German troops would occupy it. Many people pointed out that mountains and fortifications divided Germany from the Sudetenland but nothing divided the Sudetenland from the rest of Czechoslovakia. Once Hitler's troops had crossed the mountains nothing could stop them.

After his second visit to Germany Chamberlain broadcast a gloomy message to the British people:

Source 29.1 The men who signed the Munich Agreement. Neville Chamberlain is on the left

Source 29.2 I shall not give up the hope of a peaceful solution, or abandon my efforts for peace, as long as any chance for peace remains... But at this moment I see nothing further than I can usefully do...

For the present I ask you to await as calmly as you can the events of the next few days. As long as war has not begun there is always the hope that it may be prevented, and you know that I am going to work for peace to the last moment...

A few hours later, Chamberlain received a telegram. In it, Hitler offered 'to give a formal guarantee for the rest of Czechoslovakia'.

Chamberlain knew that time was short. It was now late evening on 27 September and Hitler had fixed 1 October as the day when his troops would enter the Sudetenland. Germany meant to go ahead even if Britain and France accepted the 'guarantee'. Their choice was between accepting Hitler's actions or declaring war.

On 29 September Chamberlain flew to Germany for the last time, and that night he and the French Prime Minister, Edouard Daladier, agreed to the German occupation of the Sudetenland. By themselves, the Czechs did not have the military strength to keep the Germans out, so their government had to accept the decision.

Source 29.3 Hitler had got what he wanted, had achieved another great conquest, without firing a shot. His prestige soared to new heights. No one who was in Germany in the days after Munich, as the writer was, can forget the rapture of the German people. They were relieved that war had been averted; they were elated and swollen with pride at Hitler's bloodless victory, not only over Czechoslovakia but over Great Britain and France. Within the short space of six months, they reminded you, Hitler had conquered Austria and the Sudetenland, adding ten million inhabitants to the Third Reich and a vast strategic territory which opened the way for German domination of south-eastern Europe. And without the loss of a single German life! With the instinct of a genius rare in German history he had divined not only the weaknesses of the smaller states in central Europe but those of the two principal western democracies, Britain and France, and forced them to bend to his will. He had invented and used with staggering success a new strategy and technique of political warfare [intimidation of foreign governments], which makes actual war unnecessary.

(W. Shirer, *The Rise and Fall of the Third Reich*, London, 1960)

In a speech to German pressman Hitler commented on the long-term and recent effects of German propaganda and political warfare:

Source 29.4 It has been necessary for me to talk of peace for decades on end. For only by repeatedly emphasising the German wish for peace... could I hope gradually to secure freedom for the German people and to provide them with the right kind of armament which has always been essential to any further moves. Such peace propaganda unavoidably has its questionable side effects. This is because it may lead many people to think that the existing régime really does want exactly what it says – to keep the peace at any costs.

It was necessary to influence [the Czech government] through the press and other means of propaganda... [According to the press] shooting was going on continuously day and night along the Czech border. Czech bunkers were being shelled incessantly... Their nerves did not stand up to it. They cracked and collapsed, and in the end we did not have to take up arms.

In Britain, as in Germany, many people were very pleased about the Munich Agreement (see source 29.7). However, a few spoke out and said how bad they thought it was:

Source 29.5 We have sustained a total and unmitigated defeat... We are in the midst of a disaster of the first magnitude. The road down the Danube... the road to the Black Sea has been opened... All the countries of [Middle Europe] and the Danube Valley, one after another, will be drawn into the vast system of

Source 29.6 Chamberlain returning home

MR. CHAMBERLAIN'S PURPOSE

Braving Europe's Antagonisms to Rescue a Generation from War Fears

ALREADY Mr. Chamberlain has returned from the Munich Conference, bringing his sheaves with him. The harvest that he has reaped is the harvest that he has sown —a harvest of peace.

His coming home has been as swift and sudden as his setting out; and in that little interval of time, measured by the quickened heart-beats of the world, the whole outlook on the future has been transformed.

In his broadcast speech on Tuesday Mr. Chamberlain professed himself a man of peace to the depth of his soul. "Armed conflict between the nations," he said, "is a nightmare to me. . . . I am going to work for peace to the last moment." He has been as good as his word, and to-day he has his reward. Out of the nettle, danger, he has plucked the flower, safety.

Source 29.7   From the *Daily Telegraph*
1 October 1938

Nazi politics... And do not suppose that this is the end. It is only the beginning.

(From a speech by Winston Churchill)

Churchill was soon proved right. Hitler's troops had occupied the Sudetenland in October 1938 as planned, and within five months they had taken over the rest of Czechoslovakia. It was clear that Hitler meant to go on expanding his territory. It was also clear that stopping him would now be hard, since Germany's size and productive power had become enormous. Czechoslovakia was a thriving industrial country and its output, added to Germany's, meant that the Nazis' capabilities for waging war exceeded those of Britain, France and the other countries of western Europe.

1   Look at source 29.4. In Hitler's view
    a) What long-term effect had his propaganda had on western governments?
    b) What effect had it had on the Czech government in 1938?

2   Why do you think nearly everyone in Britain was delighted when they heard about the Munich Agreement? Suggest one or two replies which they might have made to Churchill.

3   Look at sources 29.2 and 29.6. What attitudes do they convey?

4   Look at the photograph of Hitler in the Sudetenland on page 70 and suggest a caption which a) Goebbels and b) Churchill might have written for it.

30   Crystal Night

The Nazi persecution of Jews had intensified during the late 1930s. As a result, many Jewish families wished to emigrate. The Nazis strongly approved of this, but voluntary emigration proved to be very slow and difficult. This was partly because the Jews often lacked the money to pay for their journeys and resettlement. There was also the problem of finding new homes, since neighbouring countries also had anti-semitic governments. Palestine, in the Middle East, was the ancient home of the Jewish people, and Jews who were already living there welcomed other Jews from all over the world. However, Palestine was ruled by Britain, and Britain restricted the pace of Jewish immigration.

Because of these problems the Nazis began to deport Jews by force. They rounded up Jewish families, herded them to railway stations and padlocked them into cattle wagons for transportation to Germany's borders. Sometimes they marked the wagons with slogans like 'Danger, consignment of dirty Jews.' The wagons might be put into sidings for several days so that other trains could have priority. The families packed inside them were left without food, drink or toilet facilities. Local people sometimes crept to the sidings at night to pass some food and water through the ventilation slits in the wagons. In spite of their efforts, the people were often dead by the time the wagons arrived at their destinations. Bodies tumbled out as soon as the doors were unlocked, though whimpering children sometimes had to be dragged from the darkness. The Nazis did not mind the deaths, although their official purpose was to resettle the Jews in the countries from which they had entered Germany. Poland was one of the main destinations, and deportations to Poland reached a peak at the end of October 1938. (This was to beat a deadline set by the Polish government.)

On 7 November 1938 a German Jew who was living in Paris showed his disgust at what was happening. He went to the German Embassy and shot an official, who died two days later. Goebbels responded by ordering Nazi officials to stage 'spontaneous anti-Jewish demonstrations' throughout Germany. The following night is sometimes known as 'Crystal Night' or 'The Night of Glass' because so many windows were broken. The destruction was still going on when people awoke the next morning (10 November):

Source 30.1 Along the main street the windows of Jewish shops and department stores have been smashed, the contents looted, torn, broken up and scattered. Shop signs carrying Jewish names are being hauled down, books are burning outside the bookshops and anti-Jewish slogans are screaming from walls and hoardings next to giant Swastikas. All too visibly, storm-troopers are in command of the street, and still more are arriving in open trucks, sitting straight as boards, with tight lips and arms crossed in front of their chests...

'Out of the way!' a trooper warns me,

The Jews were fined for what had happened on 'Crystal Night', as if they had caused all the damage themselves. This, and the fact that the government seized their insurance payments, reduced many Jews to poverty.

Source 30.2
Sweeping up after 'Crystal Night'

getting ready to hurl a brick into a first-floor window. '*Jude verrecke!*' [Death to the Jews] he shouts, and glass breaks.

The sun is streaming into gaping shops, flashing on glass splinters, highlighting the yellow Jewish stars smeared on doors like the sign of the plague. Frightened by the display of violence... I turn to an elderly man who is watching from a doorway.

'Excuse me, why are they doing all this?'

'It's the Jews they're after.'

'Why, what have they done?'

The man looks at me as if I am trying to tease him with my questions.

'Nothing really,' he says at length. 'They're different, they know how to make money, they... don't they drum the lesson into your heads at school and in the Hitler Youth?'

I stay silent... In the past I have seen anti-Jewish feeling expressed only in its non-violent form: Sarah, brunette and pretty, suddenly staying away from school, and no one has seen or heard of her since; the Aryan passport which, complete with family tree and evidence of at least two pure Aryan generations, identifies the holder as a 'first-class' citizen.

The man noisily blows his nose.

'They took a lot of them away last night... burnt down their synagogue... and now all this! Poor devils!'

He shuffles away and I ride off to school without looking back, aching with what I have seen and heard and don't quite understand.

(From M. McKinnon, *The Naked Years*, London, 1987)

Source 30.3
Human misery by the trainload

In conducting their anti-Jewish campaign the Nazis met one serious problem: despite the cruel drawings used in Nazi posters, Jews were often hard to identify. The Nazis solved this problem by studying family trees; they also listed Jewish names and forced Jews to use them. Lastly, they made the Jews wear yellow stars on their clothes. The star was a symbol of the Jewish religion; now it was also a symbol of Nazi cruelty and persecution. Other 'undesirable' groups in German society also had to wear special badges; for example, homosexuals had to wear a pink triangle.

Source 30.4

This cartoon shows swastikas raining down on some people

Hagelschauern

Gott der Gerechte, warum haft Du uns verlassen

Using the Evidence

1 Goebbels called for 'spontaneous anti-Jewish demonstrations'. What did he really mean by 'spontaneous'?

2 Study source 30.1. What do we know about the writer at the time she saw the events? Roughly how long afterwards was the source published? How do these factors affect its value as evidence?

3 Why does the writer describe the way the storm-troopers were sitting? Why do you think she mentions the way the man blew his nose?

4 How did the writer feel about what she witnessed? How can you tell?

5 What event in the writer's childhood seemed non-violent at the time? What does she probably think about it now?

31 Pressure on Poland

Under the Treaty of Versailles, Germany had had to give up the area known as Poland. It became an independent country, and its boundaries were drawn so that it included the strip of land (called the 'Polish corridor') which cut East Prussia off from the rest of Germany. In addition, the German city of Danzig was placed under international control, and the Poles had special privileges there. For the Germans these were among the most hated parts of the Treaty.

Source 31.1 Poland's existence is intolerable and incompatible with the essential conditions of Germany's life. Poland must go and will go... The obliteration of Poland must be one of the fundamental drives of German policy.

(General von Seekt in 1922)

Ideas like this, coupled with Hitler's hatred of the Slavs and his wish for 'living space' in central Europe, showed that the threat to Poland was very severe indeed.

In October 1938 the Germans began to put pressure on the Poles. They said they wanted to build a railway and a motorway across the 'Polish corridor' to link the two parts of Germany. They also demanded the return of Danzig to German control.

The Poles were prepared to consider the road and railway links but refused the German demands over Danzig. They showed their determination by issuing guns to Polish customs officers in the city. These would help them to deal with German gunrunners and other military personnel who were entering Danzig in growing numbers.

In the following March the Germans made military threats against the tiny country of Lithuania, forcing it to give up Memel, another region which Germany had lost under the Treaty of Versailles. There could now be no doubt that the Germans would soon increase their efforts to regain Danzig – and possibly parts of Poland, too. According to the German press, Germans living in Poland were being persecuted. Similar reports had appeared just before the military action in Austria and Czechoslovakia, and the new reports sharpened fears of a German invasion of Poland. The Poles were right to be apprehensive, since the Nazis were drawing up secret plans to invade in the autumn.

The American President, Franklin Roosevelt,

felt that international pressure might discourage Hitler from going to war. He therefore drew up a list of 31 countries which were in Europe and around the Mediterranean Sea. He announced that he was sending the list to Hitler and demanding guarantees that Germany had no intention of attacking these countries. Although Hitler's word could not be trusted Roosevelt felt that this was a way to embarrass him and to make the rest of the world more wary of what he was doing. Hitler responded by asking all the countries except Poland, Russia, Britain and France whether they felt threatened by Germany and whether they had asked Roosevelt to speak on their behalf. Most of the countries said no to both questions, and Hitler used this to make Roosevelt look rather foolish. He announced the · result of his survey in a brilliant speech which was full of sarcastic jibes at American policy.

The speech was reported and published in many parts of the world. Once again Hitler was winning the propaganda war. Behind the scenes he was also achieving success in negotiations with Russia. They secretly agreed on how they might divide Poland between them.

The Nazis hated Russia's Communist system, but better relations between their countries suited the Nazi's military plans. Poland was almost surrounded by German and Russian territory. This meant that German and Russian troops could quickly close in on every side and win an easy victory. Speed was important to Hitler because he feared that the British and French would at last try to put a stop to his empire-building. If so he might have to deal with a British and French attack in western Europe. He could not afford to have troops bogged down in a lengthy campaign on the opposite side of the continent.

On 31 August 1939 a number of incidents occurred along the German-Polish border. A German soldier later described the part he had played in one rather puzzling 'attack' that night:

Source 31.2 In order to carry out this attack I had to apply... for the 'Canned Goods'... I received this man and had him laid down near the entrance to the [radio] station. He was alive but completely unconscious. I tried to open his eyes. I could not tell by his eyes that he was alive, only by his breathing. I could not see the gun wounds but a lot of blood was smeared across his face. He was in civilian clothes.

We seized the radio station, as ordered, broadcast over the emergency transmitter a speech in Polish stating that the time had come for conflict between the Germans and Poles, fired some pistol shots and left.

(Edited from an affidavit by A. Naujocks (Nuremberg documents))

Source 31.3 Winston Churchill. After Chamberlain's death in 1940, Churchill, who had taken over as Prime Minister, said, 'It fell to Neville Chamberlain in one of the supreme crises of the world to be contradicted by events, to be disappointed in his hopes and to be deceived and cheated by a wicked man.' (From a speech in the House of Commons, November 12, 1940)

Using the Evidence

1 Why do you think the Nazis claimed that Germans living in Poland were being persecuted?

2 Look at source 31.2. What did the code name 'Canned Goods' stand for?

3 Suggest where the victim might have come from. What might have been done to make him unconscious?

4 What did the Germans want people to think had happened at the transmitter, which was just inside the German border?

5 What was the point of staging incidents of this kind?

Coursework

Compare two accounts of a single incident. (You could use newspapers, or you could get friends to write reports about an incident in your school or town. If necessary, you could write one of the reports yourself and get the other from someone who disagrees about some of the details.) Carefully study the differences between the reports then try to explain how they came about.

There are several cases in this book where people saw the same thing differently. Choose an example and see if you can account for some of the differences.

32 Europe at War

Source 32.1 He gave his word that he neither wished nor intended to annex Austria; he broke it. He declared that he would not incorporate the Czechs in the Reich; he did so. He gave his word after Munich that he had no further territorial demands in Europe; he broke it. He gave his word that he wanted no Polish provinces; he broke it. He has sworn to you for years that he was the natural enemy of Bolshevism; he is now its ally.

Can you wonder his word is, for us, not worth the paper it is written on?

(Documents concerning German-Polish relations and the outbreak of hostilities..., HMSO, 1939)

Source 32.2

The Nazi war machine crushing Poland

NEXT!

August 24, 1939

Source 32.1 is part of a broadcast which Neville Chamberlain made to the Germans on 4 September 1939. Three days earlier Hitler's troops and air force had invaded Poland. Their rapid, mechanised onslaught is known by the German name of *blitzkrieg*, meaning 'lightning war'. For the first time in history, bomber aircraft destroyed towns and cities, while tanks rolled across the open country. As German troops were overrunning western Poland Russian troops were preparing to enter from the east, in accordance with the Russian-German treaties.

On 3 September Britain and France had declared war on Germany. However, they did not attempt to help Poland; instead, nearly all their troops remained in Britain and France, hoping to fight off a German attack. By the end of October the Germans and Russians had conquered Poland, and within six months Denmark, Norway, Holland, Belgium, Luxembourg and France had fallen under German control. Britain was now the obvious target but the North Sea and the English Channel protected it from the Germans' favourite weapon, the tank. Germany planned to invade by sea after first destroying the British Air Force. Sudden attacks by German bombers had destroyed most of Poland's fighters before they could leave the ground. The Germans hoped to destroy the British Air Force in a similar way, and in the summer of 1940 German bombers struck at British airfields. However, the British, using their newly-invented radar, detected the waves of approaching German bombers in plenty of time. They were therefore able to get their fighters off the ground and meet the Germans in the air. This phase of the war, called the Battle of Britain, lasted for about two months. It resulted in heavy German losses but left the British Air Force with sufficient strength to deal with any attempted landing.

The Germans abandoned their plans for an autumn invasion of Britain. Instead, they increased their efforts to demoralise and starve the British. They bombed British cities and intensified their U-boat (or submarine) campaign, which was aimed against ships bringing food and equipment across the Atlantic.

More important, they turned their attention to eastern Europe again. France was defeated and Britain was powerless to launch an attack so the Germans now had no need to fear a war on two fronts. They, therefore, broke their treaties with Russia and launched a blitzkrieg across the Russian-held part of Poland and deep into Russia itself. However, in a giant country like Russia the German drive quickly ran out of strength.

By the end of 1941 the Germans had come to a standstill along a front which stretched from Leningrad in the north to Rostov in the south. Midway, they were within 50 kilometres of Moscow, the Russian capital. The Russian winter closed in. It was so severe that German convoys sometimes disappeared under snowdrifts. The poor state of Russian roads helped to make things worse for the Germans. Vehicles sometimes sank in mud which froze round the wheels, locking them in place for weeks or even months. As the cold grew worse a number of German soldiers died of frostbite and pneumonia. Hot drinks froze in flasks and soldiers sometimes froze at their posts.

In the spring of 1942 the Germans tried to push further into Russia, and they had some successes in the south. However, the city of Stalingrad held out for weeks:

Source 32.3 Eighty days and eighty nights of hand-to-hand struggles. The street is no longer measured by metres but by corpses... Stalingrad is no longer a town. By day it is an enormous cloud of burning, blinding smoke; it is a vast furnace, lit by the reflection of the flames. And when the night arrives, one of those scorching, howling, bleeding nights, the dogs plunge into the Volga and swim desperately to gain the other bank. The nights in Stalingrad are a terror for them. Animals flee this hell; the hardest stones cannot bear it for long; only men endure.

(A German Lieutenant quoted in J. Hamer, *The Twentieth Century*, London, 1980)

In the end the Germans took Stalingrad but Russian troops then trapped them there and defeated them among the ruins. Further north the Russians began to push them towards Germany, and another winter added to the Germans' problems.

The German campaign in Russia had weakened the Germans very severely indeed. Up to 1941 the Russians had sold the Germans a wide range of products and raw materials. The Russians cut off all supplies when the Germans attacked but the Germans planned to plunder the occupied territories and take what they wanted. The Russians foiled the Germans' plans by destroying or removing the means of production. As the Germans advanced, manufacturing plant was transported eastwards to places well beyond the war zone. The Russians then set it up again and continued to use it. Thus, although they gained Russian territory the Germans went short of vital supplies. The campaign also cost them tanks, aircraft and up to a million fighting men.

THE DRAGON-SLAYER
"So much for that one, and now to face the next."

Source 32.4

A cartoon based on the idea of St George and the dragon

Source 32.5   Russians defending Moscow

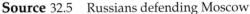

Using the Evidence

1   Look at source 32.1. Why did Chamberlain say that Hitler was now an ally of Bolshevism?

2   Why do you think he wanted to speak to the German people?

3   Look at source 32.2. What aspect of Germany's war with Poland was the artist concentrating on?

4   Look at sources 31.3 and 32.4. Suggest what the cartoonist was saying.
    Do you think the cartoon appeared in Britain or Germany? Why?

5   Why did Hitler feel safe to turn on Russia in 1941? What went wrong for the Germans?

Coursework

In 1938 a film called *Inside Nazi Germany* had been banned from British cinemas because 'it might offend... a friendly nation' (Germany).

What does this say about freedom in Britain at that time? What good or harm might the ban have done? Discuss the arguments for and against such censorship.

---

33 The Final Solution

In the 1930s the Nazis had set up prison, or concentration camps for those who opposed them. By the end of 1938 they had started to fill them with Jews and other 'undesirables'. As the Nazis seized new parts of Europe the number of Jewish victims increased, and Jews were snatched from towns and villages right across Europe. Now the Nazis introduced their 'final solution':

Source 33.1 In the course of the final solution, the Jews should be brought under appropriate direction in a suitable manner to the east for labour utilisation. Separated by sex, the Jews capable of work will be led into these areas in large labour columns to build roads, whereby doubtless a large part will fall away through natural reduction.

The inevitable final remainder... will have to be dealt with appropriately.

(R. Heydrich, speaking from a draft prepared by K.A. Eichmann, who was in charge of the Jewish Office of the Gestapo (the German Secret Police))

As this shows, the 'final solution' involved mass murder, but it also involved exploiting the victims as much as possible in the process.

Throughout the early 1940s trainloads of Jewish and Gypsy victims arrived at the concentration camps each day. Besides being marched from the camps to build roads the victims had to work in factories on the sites, thus keeping the Nazis supplied with war materials. The Nazis soon had more slave labour than they could use. Eichmann had already planned to execute those who could not be worked to death, and 'murder camps' were set up at various places in Poland. The most notorious camp was the one at Auschwitz, which was equipped to dispose of its victims on an industrial scale. On arrival, the most able-bodied people were picked for slave labour. The rest, including mothers, children, and those who were sick or elderly, had to get undressed for 'disinfection'. Then they were pushed into airtight chambers and poisoned with insecticide

Source 33.2

Some of the victims inside a 'death camp'

or other gas. After ten or fifteen minutes the Nazis opened the doors and removed the victims. Most were dead; all were cremated in special ovens.

Up to 2000 people were poisoned at a time, and batch after batch were herded into the so-called 'corpse cellars' all day long. In a six-week period at the start of 1945 the Nazis at Auschwitz sent the following home to Germany:

222 000 sets of men's clothing;
193 000 sets of women's clothing;
100 000 sets of children's clothing.

They also saved the victims' glasses. They tore the rings from their fingers and prized gold fillings from their teeth. Skin (especially tattooed skin) was sometimes saved and used to make table lamps.

The Nazis' 'final solution' involved about 6 000 000 murders.

Source 33.3 Victims arriving at Auschwitz

1   Look at source 33.1. It uses expressions like 'final solution', 'appropriate direction' and 'suitable manner' to describe what is being planned for the Jews. Why do you think Eichmann 'toned down' his language in such a way?

2   Look at the last few lines of the source (from 'doubtless' onwards) and rewrite it in a way which makes Eichmann's meaning perfectly clear.

3   Tricks with language are important because they trick people's minds. The Nazis were always playing these tricks, and their clever use of language made the murder of Jews sound acceptable. Source 33.1 shows one of the ways in which they did this, but they also had another technique. Study source 8.4 and say what it is. How could language like this affect people's treatment of other races?

4   Find the word 'knives' near the end of source 20.1. Some years later, Solmitz added, 'Who took that seriously then?' How do you think her attitude to the Nazis had changed? How do you think she felt when she re-read the things she had written at the start of 1933?

34   The White Rose Letters

Hitler's unwise Russian campaign helped to turn many German people against him. They realised that he was a power-mad and irresponsible man who ought to be stopped. By this time there were no large groups which could organise any national resistance; trades unions had been banned and so had political parties (apart from the Nazi Party). Resistance by the Church had been stamped out and the curbs on free speech made it hard for anti-Hitler groups to attract new supporters. Sometimes they did not even know of each other's existence. Most opposition was therefore carried on in underground groups or 'cells', often with no more than 12 or 20 members each. There were many such groups, and their number and secrecy meant that they were a serious threat to Hitler and other leading Nazis.

One group was based at Munich University, which became a hotbed of student unrest as the German army retreated from Russia. The students were smuggling anti-Nazi leaflets (known as 'White Rose Letters') to other universities. To deal with the problem a Nazi official went to the University with a squad of Gestapo (secret police) and SS bodyguards.

After threatening the students he began to insult them. For example, he said that the women should give up their studies and their political activities. Instead, they should serve the country by going to bed with soldiers and having babies. His insults angered the students so much that they threw their unwanted visitors out. Then they marched through the streets of Munich calling on Germans to rise against the Nazis. No one had dared to do such a thing for many years, and the Gestapo tried to find out who the ringleaders were. A few days later a brother and sister called Hans and Sophie Scholl were seen flinging leaflets from a balcony, and the Gestapo arrested them. They were tortured, tried and put to death. Sophie Scholl, whose leg had been broken, had to limp to the scaffold on crutches. Other members of the University were also hanged for their anti-Nazi activities, which were classed as treason.

The following source comes from one of the leaflets which Hans and Sophie Scholl distributed:

Source 34.1 Fellow students!
The nation is profoundly shaken by the defeat

of our troops at Stalingrad. Three hundred and thirty thousand Germans have been senselessly and irresponsibly led to death and destruction through the cunning strategy of a corporal from World War 1. Our Führer, we thank you!

The German people are growing restive. Are we to go on handing over the fate of our armies to an amateur? ... Never. The time is coming for the youth of Germany to settle accounts with the most loathsome tyranny ever to fall upon our people. In the name of German youth we demand from this Adolf Hitler's Government the return of our personal freedom, our most treasured possession which has been filched from us in a most despicable way.

We have grown up in a state which has ruthlessly muzzled every free expression of opinion. During the critical years of our development the Hitler Youth, the SA and the SS have tried to regiment us, to revolutionise us, to dope us... They drown in a flood of empty phrases all our attempts to think for ourselves... Those of us who work with our minds will of course be expected to twist everything into the service of this new race of masters.

Party officials are free to make a shameless mockery of the honour of our female students. German women of the University of Munich gave the right answer to that sort of smearing of their honour; indeed, German students have stood up in defence of their colleagues.

For us there can be only one cry. Fight against the Party! Give up your membership of Party organisations... Quit courses offered by SS leaders or other Party stooges! ... We will not be terrified by threats, no, not even by the threat to close the universities. This is something which concerns every single one of us now and in the future: our freedom and honour as members of a morally responsible nation.

Source 34.2
One of the leaflets which Hans and Sophie Scholl distributed

Source 34.2 Little German girls attend a party celebration in Coburg. From earliest childhood the German children were taught in the classroom to deify the Fuhrer, to greet each other with 'Heil Hitler' and to swear alliegance to him

1 Study source 34.1. Which corporal from World War 1 does it mention?

2 How does the leaflet explain the defeat at Stalingrad? Why does it say, 'Our Führer, we thank you!'?

3 Was the leaflet produced before or after the Nazi official visited the University? How can you tell?

4 Why do you think the Nazis wanted a rise in the birth-rate?

5 Why might they have regretted breaking Sophie Scholl's leg?

6 What was the Scholls' main complaint about the Nazis? What evidence in this book could be used to support their complaint?

7 How did the Scholls feel about scenes like the one in source 34.3? How can you tell?

35 The Stauffenberg Bomb Plot

Some opposition groups planned to murder Hitler. They felt that this was the only way to put an end to the War and the concentration camps. They also felt that Germany must either make peace quickly or suffer defeat and humiliation. Total defeat could lead to an even more severe treaty than the one which had followed the First World War. The groups knew that Hitler would never make peace; his desire to fight was far too strong and a mental illness was clouding his judgment. In any case, Germany's enemies would not be prepared to negotiate with him.

A further reason for killing Hitler was to show other countries that many Germans opposed his rule. Only in this way would Germans gain the respect and sympathy they deserved. Throughout the War the foreign press had carried stories of German crimes, but the plotters felt that most of the German public were blameless. The Jews, Poles, Czechs, Russians and other peoples had suffered at the hands of the Nazi leaders; most of the German nation were victims like everyone else. Killing Hitler would not simply get him out of the way; it would also show the rest of the world that the Germans valued peace and democracy and had a right to discuss their own future.

Among the people who plotted against Hitler were members of the German Forces Intelligence Bureau, known as the *Abwehr*. On one occasion they planted a bomb on his aircraft but it failed to explode. On another occasion a brave conspirator with his pockets full of explosives tried unsuccessfully to get near to Hitler to blow him up. Although these plots were never discovered Hitler sensed danger. At the start of 1944 he abolished the Abwehr, but some of its leading members continued to plot against him. Their most dramatic attempt on his life was the Stauffenberg Bomb Plot of July 1944. Hitler was now spending much of his time at a fortified hideaway in East Prussia known as the Wolf's Lair.

In July 1944 Hitler ordered a colonel called von Stauffenberg to come to the Wolf's Lair for military briefings. Von Stauffenberg had already taken part in Abwehr plots against Hitler and he felt that this was an ideal chance to make another attempt on his life. During the meeting, Stauffenberg placed his briefcase on the floor near the leg of Hitler's table. He then left the room 'to make an urgent telephone call'. Almost at once a bomb in the briefcase exploded. The room was wrecked but Hitler was only slightly hurt. According to German radio 'Hitler received slight burns and concussion but no injuries. He at once began to work again. He then received Mussolini for a long meeting as previously arranged. There is nobody in Germany who does not feel a sense of deep gratitude that the Führer has escaped uninjured.' A few hours later he broadcast a message to the German people:

Source 35.1 My German comrades!
I speak to you today in order that you should hear my voice and know that I am unhurt and well... I regard this as a confirmation of the task imposed upon me by Providence.

Source 35.2 Inspecting the wreckage

The circle of the upstarts is very small and has nothing in common with the spirit of the German Army... or the German people. It is a gang of criminal elements which will be destroyed without mercy... This time we shall settle accounts with them in the manner to which we National Socialists are accustomed.

Believing that Hitler must have been killed, Stauffenberg and other conspirators had tried to set up a new German government. However, they had been arrested and executed by the time Hitler spoke. His threats were aimed at conspirators who had not been caught and also at other opponents, mainly army officers. In the next few weeks the Gestapo arrested thousands of officers, and most of them were tried and hanged. Goebbels had one of the main trials filmed, and the officers were not allowed to wear their uniforms. Instead, they had to wear shabby jackets and ill-fitting trousers without belts or braces. One man had his false teeth taken away before the trial began. He had to keep grasping his trousers to stop them falling down, and the judge shouted at him, 'You dirty old man. Why don't you leave your trousers alone?'

The victims of Hitler's 'purge' included a man called von Moltke, who had led a secret discussion group. Moltke owned a large estate at Kraisau in Prussia, and the group was called the Kraisau Circle. The members had spent many hours in trying to work out a new political system for post-War Germany and Europe. They did not plot against Nazi rule but they longed for its replacement by a gentler, democratic form of government.

Members of the Circle had been in touch with British representatives. Like other groups, they wanted to guard against Germany being treated as a criminal nation after the War, and they emphasised that the German masses should not be blamed for the Nazis' crimes.

The Circle had done its best to keep its activities secret. The members had met in a wide range of places – mostly their homes. They had burned unwanted documents and kept the most important ones in a beehive on Von Moltke's estate. Despite these precautions the Gestapo found out what they were doing and rounded up nearly all the members. Just before his execution Moltke wrote to his wife, 'We are all to be hanged for thinking together.'

1 Look at chapter 32. What evidence is there that Germany's enemies would not be prepared to negotiate with Hitler?

2 According to one writer, after the explosion Hitler staggered out of the Wolf's Lair with 'his face blackened, his hair smouldering and his trousers in shreds.' Do you think this writer was a supporter or an opponent of Hitler? Why do you think so?

3 How does the radio broadcast deal with this incident?

4 Study source 35.1. How did Hitler account for his lucky escape? Why did he bother to mention this?

5 Hitler could have condemned the German nation for being full of traitors. What did he do instead?

6 Why do you think Goebbels had one of the main trials filmed? Why were the officers made to appear in ill-fitting clothes?

36 The End of Nazi Germany

In December 1941 Germany had declared war on the United States. There were two main reasons for the German move. Firstly, Germany resented the fact that America was sending Britain and Russia weapons and other war supplies. Secondly, Germany wanted to support its ally, Japan, which had just begun a war with America in the Pacific Ocean. Fighting was now affecting many parts of the world, and the global conflict is usually known as the Second World War.

The Germans were already at war with the world's largest country, Russia, and now they had challenged its wealthiest country, the United States. They may have thought that its war with Japan would prevent America from increasing its involvement in Europe. However, the United States began to establish military bases in Britain, and Britain and America prepared to invade and liberate the Nazi-held countries of western Europe. The invasion took place on 6 June 1944. British and American troops were landed in northern France and France was freed from Nazi control. British, French and American troops then fought their way into Germany. By the start of 1945 they were advancing across the western half of Hitler's Reich, while Russian troops advanced from the east. On 25 April the Americans and Russians met at a place called Torgau, 130 kilometres south of Berlin. They also met in other parts of central Europe as they liberated other countries from Nazi control. The Nazis still had control of Berlin but Russian troops were closing in.

Source 36.1

Now very ill, Hitler remained in a bunker beneath the Chancellery building, clinging to the hope that Germany would somehow survive. At last, on 18 April, he began to prepare for defeat and death. His mistress had joined him in the bunker, and that night they were formally married, declaring that they were 'of Aryan descent' and had 'no hereditary diseases'. They then tried to celebrate by drinking champagne, which slopped in the glasses as Russian bombs exploded nearby.

Hitler spent the early hours of 29 April dictating two famous documents, his will and his political testament (final statement). In his will he said that he and his wife had chosen suicide rather than defeat. They killed themselves on the following day and their bodies were burned with petrol in the Chancellery garden, though no remains have ever been found. The political testament shows how firmly Hitler had stuck to his views on race:

Source 36.3 More than thirty years have now passed since in 1914 I made my modest contribution as a volunteer in the First World War that was forced upon the Reich. In these decades I have acted solely out of love and loyalty to my people in all my thoughts, acts and life...

It is untrue that I or anyone else in Germany wanted a war in 1939. It was desired and instigated exclusively by those international statesmen who were either of Jewish descent or worked for Jewish interests... Above all else, I charge the leaders of the nation and those under them to scrupulous observance of the laws of race and to merciless opposition to the universal poisoner of all peoples, International Jewry.

Source 36.2

Source 36.4 The mass grave of concentration camp victims

On 7 May Germany surrendered to the Americans and their allies. It was divided up into British, French, American and Russian zones, and Berlin (inside the Russian zone) was divided up in a similar way. The four main zones were roughly the same as the areas which the victorious armies had occupied. Like Hitler, Nazi Germany no longer existed.

_____ **Using the Evidence** _____

1 Look at source 36.1. What do you think it shows?
2 Source 36.2 was taken in Berlin and shows the Russian flag. What do you think is happening?
3 Look at source 36.4 and consider Hitler's claim to have acted out of love and loyalty to his people. Which groups did the Nazis reject or treat with disrespect? Who did they accept as equals?

_____ **Coursework** _____

List some of the factors which helped the Nazis to come to power and some of the factors which caused their defeat. What lessons can we learn from what happened in Germany?

Although they were allies during the War, America and Russia soon began to compete with each other. They came to be known as the Superpowers because of the way they brought other countries under their influence. This was clearly seen in Europe, where the Superpowers set up rival military bases in the countries they had freed from the Nazis. The British, French and American zones of Germany were combined to form West Germany (with American bases), while the Russian zone became East Germany (with Russian bases). The division of Germany was felt most sharply in Berlin. The British, French and American zones were combined to form West Berlin, but the Russian zone remained separate. Known as East Berlin, it was closely linked with East Germany but in 1961 its links with the rest of Berlin were cut. This occurred when Khrushchev (the Russian leader) ordered the building of the Berlin Wall along the boundary through the city centre.

In western Europe some people already spoke of an iron curtain of secrecy dividing the two halves of Europe. The guarded and fortified Wall seemed to give this curtain visible form. East Germany's border with West Germany was already closed but East Germans had been able to enter West Berlin and fly from there to West Germany. Now they had no way of reaching the West, and many German families were split. Some people tunnelled under the Wall or scrambled over it, though they risked being shot.

At last, in 1989, openings were made in the Berlin Wall and people were once again free to pass through. Many Berliners were overjoyed that this had occurred, and hopes were raised throughout the two halves of Germany that the country would soon be reunited.

East Germans pass to the West through a crossing point in the Wall that has just been opened

Russia's present leader, Mr. Gorbachev on a visit to West Germany

Coursework

In 1945, troops from east and west met roughly along a line from Lübeck (in Germany) to Trieste (now in Italy). Use an atlas to find out which countries lie to the east and west of this division. Your atlas will probably show which countries belong to the American-led military alliance called the North Atlantic Treaty Organisation (NATO), formed in 1949, and which belong to the Russian-led military alliance called the Warsaw Pact, formed in 1955. It may also show other groupings, such as the European Economic Community and its Russian-led equivalent, the Council for Mutual Economic Aid (Comecon). To what extent do these current groupings reflect the division of Europe in 1945? How does this apply to Germany?

Further Reading

C. Cross, *The British at War*, Observer and C I Audio Visual Ltd., n.d. (A colour slide sound programme relating to both world wars)

A. Frank, *The Diary of Anne Frank*, Pan Books, 1954

R. Garrett, *Kaiser Bill*, Wayland, 1978

A. Hitler, *Mein Kampf*, tr. R. Manheim, Hutchinson, 1980

A. de Jonge, *The Weimar Chronicle*, Paddington Press, 1978

J. McKenzie, *Weimar Germany 1918–1933*, Blandford, 1971

J. Noakes and G. Pridham, *Documents on Nazism 1919–1945*, Cape, 1974

R. Parkinson, *The Origins of World War II*, Wayland, 1970

R. Procktor, *Nazi Germany*, Bodley Head, 1970

M. A. Puller Smith, *Hitler and Mussolini: The Western Dictators*, Blackie, 1978

W. Shirer, *The Rise and Fall of the Third Reich*, Pan Books, 1960 (and other editions)

A. Stichting, *Anne Frank in the World*, Amsterdam, 1985

R. Stone, *The Drift to War*, Heinemann Educational Books, 1976

S. Taylor, *Revolution, Counter-revolution and the Rise of Hitler*, Duckworth, 1983

R. Wolfson, *From Peace to War: European Relations 1919–1939*, E. Arnold, 1981

Acknowledgements

The author and publishers would like to acknowledge, with thanks, the following photographic sources:

American Library of Congress: p. 26; BPCC: pp. 4, 5, 37, 77; Bundesarchiv: p. 40; *Daily Telegraph*: p. 73; Hulton Picture Company: pp. 7, 8, 9, 12 (bottom), 14 (bottom), 30 (centre), 42, 43, 52, 58, 59, 70, 72 (bottom); Imperial War Museum: pp. 54, 66, 68, 71, 82, 86 (right), 91; David Low & Mail Newspapers PLC: p. 56; Novosti: p. 90; Popperfoto: pp. 79, 92, 93; Punch Publications Ltd: pp. 4 (left), 44, 81; Suddeutscher: pp. 6 (2), 10 (3), 12 (top right), 14 (top right), 19, 21, 22, 24 (left), 31, 40, 49 (bottom), 61, 89; Ullstein: pp. 11, 18, 20, 29, 30 (bottom right), 35, 47, 49 (top right), 63, 80, 88; Wiener Library: pp. 24 (right), 53, 62, 75, 76, 83, 84, 86; *Yorkshire Post*: pp. 64–5.

We are also grateful to the following for permission to reproduce extracts from:

J. Noakes & G. Pridham (eds), *Documents on Nazism*, Jonathan Cape, 1974: pp. 51–2; N. Richardson, *The Third Reich*, Dryad Press Ltd, 1987: pp. 15, 24, 36, 37, 38, 45, 51, 52, 54; R. Morgan (ed.), *Germany 1870–1970*, BBC/Macdonald, 1970: p. 23; D. Hart Davis, *Hitler's Olympics*, Century Hutchinson, 1986: p. 58; M. McKinnon, *The Naked Years*, Chatto & Windus, 1987: pp. 74–6; P. Liddle, *Testimony of War*, M. Russel, 1979: p. 7; Alex de Jonge, *The Weimar Chronicle*, Paddington Press, 1978: pp. 21, 31, 34–5; William Shirer, *The Rise and Fall of the Third Reich*, Secker & Warburg, 1960: pp. 48, 51, 55–6, 61, 67, 68–9, 72

Designed and illustrated by Cauldron Design Studio

Index